CASTLES

AND CASTLE TOWNS OF
GREAT BRITAIN

The keep of Raglan Castle, Monmouthshire.

CASTLES
AND CASTLE TOWNS OF
GREAT BRITAIN

DAVID MOUNTFIELD

BRACKEN BOOKS
LONDON

First published in 1993 by Studio Editions Ltd, Princess House,
50 Eastcastle Street, London W1N 7AP, England.

This edition published in 1995 by Bracken Books, an imprint of
Studio Editions Ltd, Princess House, 50 Eastcastle Street,
London W1N 7AP, England.

Copyright © this edition Studio Editions Ltd, 1995

ISBN 1 85891 257 1

Printed and bound in Dubai, U.A.E

CONTENTS

Warwick Castle

Aerial view of Leeds Castle, acclaimed as the most romantic castle in England.

INTRODUCTION

The medieval castle served many purposes, but essentially it was both a military stronghold and a residence. It provided a base where the lord and his retainers were relatively safe from attack and from which they could sally forth to assault invading enemies or rebellious peasants—or in some lamentable cases to indulge in rape and pillage. As it was also the lord's residence, it was a seat of local government, where justice was administered, criminals imprisoned, weapons stored, records kept, retainers feasted and dozens of other social and political functions carried out. Many castles were far more significant in this continuing administrative role than for their sporadic military engagements, but because the surviving ruins are generally of their defensive structures, we tend to think of castles primarily in terms of battles and sieges.

There are some famous stories of successful sieges, notably at Bedford, Rochester (p 104), and—a tremendous epic—at Château Gaillard in Normandy, which was captured by King Philip II of France in 1204. But these campaigns are famous partly because their successful result was so rare. Castles were not very often captured by direct assault, even by mining, which was much the most effective form of attack. They generally surrendered after a prolonged siege, with no prospect of immediate relief, and while decent surrender terms could still be negotiated. Garrisons were often remarkably small. A few dozen determined men could hold a well-built castle against much larger forces, and some castles survived the centuries without ever having to endure a siege at all.

Many have lasted to this day, a few still serving as private residences, but the majority have succumbed to the long siege of time and neglect. Their ruins have attracted sightseers in growing numbers since the eighteenth century, and today nearly all are preserved by state or other institutions (a diminishing number by their hard-pressed private own-

ers). They appear at their most romantic in prints of the eighteenth and nineteenth centuries, such as those reproduced in this book. But, like the dinosaurs, castles are perhaps most to be admired now they are long extinct. However charming they look with swans swimming among the lilies in the moat and wild honeysuckle climbing over the fallen battlements, they are relics of an age when life was nastier, more brutish and very often much shorter.

The great age of castle building roughly coincided with the form of social organization that we call feudalism, of which the castle was a physical expression. In England and Wales this lasted from the late eleventh to the fifteenth centuries, beginning about a century later in Ireland and continuing about a century longer in Scotland. In lawless times and remote places, it was necessary for any man of property to take measures to defend what he owned, but not all of the great profusion of tower houses, peel towers, and similar structures common in Scotland, Ireland and northern England, can really be classed as castles. Their purpose was to guard against sudden raids by hostile but ill-armed neighbours or tenants, not to withstand attack by an army.

However, the name 'castle', like the French *château*, does not necessarily describe a fortified residence of any kind. It is often applied to palaces and country houses that couldn't keep out a burglar, never mind an army. Besides these Classical residences, sham castles were built as early as the seventeenth century, and the nostalgic medievalism of the nineteenth century resulted in the construction of a substantial number of mansions in the more or less convincing form of medieval castles, culminating in Sir Edwin Lutyens's 'Norman' Castle Drogo, in Devon, which was built in the 1920s. None of these qualify.

Castles were built at strategically important sites, such as a port, a river crossing, or a hill pass. They might be in or close to a pre-existing town or, less often, far removed from any large habitation. William the Conqueror's primary purpose for building the Tower of London (p 114) was to inhibit violent expressions of dissatisfaction by Londoners, but he built Windsor (p 122) as one of a ring of fortresses roughly equidistant from the capital and designed to defend its approaches—in Windsor's case along the line of the Thames valley. The Tower had the Londoners at its gate (dwellings had to be pulled down to allow the Tower to expand), whereas at Windsor the site chosen was over two miles away from the village of that name, with the result that an extirely new settlement, 'New Windsor', grew up around the castle.

Though castles were largely self-sufficient, they naturally demanded supplies and services from outside, and therefore attracted settlements and encouraged urban growth (in Germany the name *Burg*, meaning 'castle', came to be applied also to the associated town). They also provided shelter for the citizens in time of war. The castles that arose so rapidly after the Norman Conquest of the eleventh century were no doubt regarded as hateful instruments of alien oppression, but in later times they were more often—not always—a reassurance and a refuge. At Caernarvon (p 34) and Conwy (p 54), where again alien rule was being imposed on a potentially hostile population, the defensive walls of the castle were extended to include the town also. This may have been a deliberate attempt to associate the local people more closely with the English regime in Wales.

Extending the walls also solved what must have been a serious problem of overcrowding. At the best of times, living space in a medieval castle was constricted (the plumbing, however, wasn't always as bad as today's visitors might suppose, and a reliable internal water supply was one of the first fundamentals). In bad times the castle was even more crowded. It is hard to imagine how a large number of extra bodies, sometimes including livestock, could have been crammed in. Temporary buildings could be put up in the bailey, or courtyard, and the

refugees no doubt brought in food supplies of their own, but a long siege would make conditions intolerable unless, as often happened, the besieging force agreed to let civilians pass through their ranks. Otherwise the unfortunate townsfolk might be expelled by the castle's commander and stranded in no-man's-land between the castle and the lines of the attackers; 400 people died of starvation in the winter of 1203–4 when this happened during the siege of Château Gaillard.

At the time of the Norman Conquest in 1066 there were virtually no castles in England, their absence making life much easier for the conquerors. There were fortifications, naturally, but they protected towns rather than residences. The invaders wished to protect not the towns, but themselves, and they threw up castles at remarkable speed—about 100 by the time of the Domesday survey less than twenty years later, about 200 by the end of the eleventh century.

Although we think of the Normans as great builders in stone, nearly all early Norman castles were built of earth and timber. This type of castle is known as 'motte and bailey' 'mound and courtyard'). It consisted of an earth mound (the tallest were about 200 feet), the excavation of which also created a ditch at its foot, with an adjoining courtyard surrounded by an earth-backed palisade. The mound was surmounted by a wooden tower, generally at least three storeys high; the bailey contained domestic buildings, stables, workshops, and so on. The shape of the bailey varied, but it was usually arranged so that no part was beyond bowshot from the tower. If an attacking force breached the bailey, the defenders took refuge in the tower on the motte.

These castles had two great advantages over stone buildings. They could be built at less cost and, more important, at much greater speed. (William the Conqueror's first castle in England, for example, was built *before* the Battle of Hastings, possibly from prefabricated parts imported from Normandy.) However, they were obviously less durable. In the few remaining examples nothing is left but the eroded earthworks, and they do not look particularly impressive now. Nevertheless, they were intimidating enough in their day. Wood, though much softer than stone, could withstand arrows and other missiles almost equally well, especially when buttressed with earth. Its main drawback was that it was all too easily set on fire. In later times, the wooden doors of stone castles manifested the same weakness.

Motte-and-bailey castles were still being built, especially in Ireland, over 100 years after the Conquest, but earlier ones were reconstructed in stone as soon as conditions permitted. Often the first stone building was a tower protecting the gate of the bailey. Wooden palisades were replaced by curtain walls. But walls, wooden or stone, are hard to defend once the attackers have actually reached them, and the 'curtain' was therefore 'hung' between projecting towers, from which fire could be brought to bear on the foot of the intervening walls. (This was a plan well known to the Romans, who indeed anticipated most of the 'advances' made by medieval castle builders.) The palisade on the mound was also often rebuilt in stone, to form the type of building known as a shell keep; Windsor is a familiar example. The old wooden towers disappeared and were replaced by a 'great tower', of the type we usually call a keep, though that name was not used by contemporaries. The Conqueror's White Tower (the Tower of London) is the best-known survivor. Sometimes it was built on the original motte, but often this was impractical because of its weight, and anyway its strength made the motte largely redundant. The great tower or keep contained the hall, the centre of the lord's household where official business was conducted, on the second storey, as well as the private apartments and chapel. These buildings tended to grow more substantial, and higher, during the twelfth century. The prize example is Dover (p 64), a great cube over ninety feet in each dimension with walls about twenty feet thick at the base.

Dover was built in the 1180s, and is rectangular, although by that time round towers were becoming more common. Cylindrical towers and round keeps had two defensive advantages: missiles tended to glance aside from the curved surface, while the lack of corners deprived enemy sappers of potential weak points to mine. From the domestic point of view, however, they were less convenient, as any lighthouse keeper would confirm. The best defence against mining was water, and a moat replaced the former dry ditch.

Dover, Henry II's masterpiece, displayed other trends, in particular the increasing importance of the gatehouse, which developed into a double tower, flanking a narrow and uninviting passage with an array of defensive arrangements—drawbridge, portcullis, 'murder holes' in the roof before the door, and so on. By 1300, some gatehouse towers were equipped with machicolation, a system of corbelled stone parapets with holes in the floor, and they were often strengthened by a barbican, a narrow, unroofed enclosure with its own gatehouse. Gatehouses eventually grew to replace the keep as the main fort-within-a-fort.

Though not planned as such, Dover may also be regarded as an early example of a 'concentric' castle, with a double curtain wall, the inner higher than the outer. This plan, probably derived from the experience of the Crusaders in the Middle East, reached its apotheosis at Beaumaris (p 22), at the beginning of the fourteenth century. Beaumaris was the last of the castles built by Edward I in North Wales in the greatest castle-building project—it is something of a mystery where the money came from—in English if not European history. In these Welsh castles the great tower or keep is absent, although it made a minor comeback later, notably at Raglan (p 98). Accommodation is provided within the gatehouse and towers of the perimeter and the hall becomes a separate building in the inner bailey.

The construction of Edward's Welsh castles was an enterprise on a national scale. Skilled workmen were hired from all over the country, from as far away as East Anglia and Northumberland, and assembled at Chester before moving to the building sites. In November, at the end of the building season, most of them went home, to be rounded up again by local sheriffs the following April. A workforce of about 1,000 was employed at Caernarvon in 1285, while half again that number were simultaneously engaged at Conwy and Harlech (p 76). At Beaumaris, built at great speed, the workforce in 1295 was over 3,000.

Those employed at Harlech during an average week in 1286 included about 250 quarrymen and stonemasons, nearly 30 carpenters and about the same number of smiths, as well as over 500 ordinary workmen. The total was swelled by guards, employed to make sure disgruntled navvies did not slip away home, and administrators of various sorts. Perhaps they included the king's chief master mason (and future Constable of Harlech), the Savoyard known as 'Master James of Saint George', whom Edward had hired when visiting his great-uncle, Philip I of Savoy, during his return from the crusade in 1272. The large number of unskilled workmen is a reminder that building a castle demanded, above all, the shifting of vast quantities of material, some of it highly intractable (at Harlech a moat was carved out of the rock).

Edward's attempts to subjugate the Scots as well as the Welsh resulted in a spate of castle-building in Scotland also around the end of the thirteenth century, but in England construction tailed off, mainly because few new castles were needed. By the late fourteenth century the role of even established castles was becoming less significant, and new castles like Bodiam (p 28) in Sussex, though still presenting a military appearance, were designed with greater concern for the comfort of the inhabitants. Changing social circumstances were making castles, if not redundant, less vital, and they played little part in the Wars of the Roses. In a way, English fifteenth-century castles owed their existence to mere habit, a castle being the natural home of a territorial magnate, and its replacement by the 'country house' was largely a development of the Renaissance. Gunpowder, however, had little to do with the decline of the castle, as early artillery was

no more effective than current siege machines. Strictly, construction of a castle, or fortification of an existing building, had always required royal permission (dozens of unauthorized castles arose in England during the 'Anarchy' of Stephen's reign, but Henry II had them all flattened). With royal authority firmly established, it was no longer necessary or desirable to allow provincial magnates to establish private strongholds. Siege warfare had already come to an end in England—though not, as it proved, permanently—before King Henry VII enacted the famous Statute of Livery and Maintenance (1487), banning the semi-professional private armies that had developed as old feudal obligations broke down. Henry also ensured that the manufacture of gunpowder, which the French demonstrated to be an effective weapon when the French army, led by Charles VIII, invaded Italy in 1494, was a royal monopoly.

The Crown had always been the largest proprietor of castles, and Henry VIII held nearly 100 of them. He was also the last royal castle builder on any scale in England, but his squat, compact, south-coast castles, such as Deal (p 6), Sandown and Walmer were essentially gun forts, which altogether lacked the political and social role of the feudal castle. Deal remains spectacularly well preserved.

Meanwhile, across England and Wales, the castles were slowly crumbling. The Civil Wars of the seventeenth century presented them with an Indian summer of sorts, but left many in ruins—less often a result of siege than of 'slighting' (dismantling) after their surrender. Some came in useful as prisons, an association which accounts for the corruption of the French word *donjon*, equivalent to what we call the keep, into the English 'dungeon'. A few castles, even massive piles like Warwick, continued to be inhabited into the present century, though the changes wrought by succeeding generations transformed them radically; old prints and paintings often reveal some of the changes. Paradoxically, the reality of a medieval building may sometimes be better appreciated from ruins than from a well-maintained castle.

The active history of the castle is longer in Scotland owing chiefly to the failure to establish a consistently strong, central government. From the end of the eleventh century, Norman lords, in this case invited by the incumbent monarch, built motte-and-bailey castles as they did in England, and in due course their successors rebuilt them in stone. The Wars of Independence produced a spate of castle building— and of castle destruction, for Robert Bruce's policy was to dismantle castles likely to be of strategic use to the English. The sequence of construction, siege, capture, destruction, recapture and reconstruction, together with the paucity of documentation, makes it impossible to say of many Lowlands castles whether they were built by the Scots or the English.

Similar doubts arise in the western Highlands and islands, where there is little evidence left of the castles that were built under Norse rule. Most of the castles in that region are relatively small and simple (medieval Scotland was a poor country) and in style tend to look earlier than they are, though that was probably a result of the need to build cheaply rather than ignorance of developments in the south.

Cost considerations also played a part in the development of the characteristically Scottish fortified residence, the tower house, which became almost universal from the fourteenth century, and many examples of which are still inhabited today. The concept of the high tower, which at one time had a semi-mystical association with lordship, continued to be popular in Scotland, while the development of what came to be called the 'Scottish baronial' style, with its plethora of spires and turrets, owed much to the *châteaux* of the Loire.

THE PLATES

Newark Castle – a major stronghold and rallying point for armies and supplies in the seventeenth century.

ALNWICK

This is the land of the Percies, guardians of the North, the allies, and occasionally rivals, of the kings of England. They bought the barony of Alnwick from the Bishop of Durham in 1309, and they still hold it today. The castle and the walled market town were then already old, and the town is said to have held a charter as a borough of King John. According to legend, however, Alnwick later incurred King John's wrath, because the roads hereabouts were so ill maintained and poorly indicated that he lost his way and fell into a bog. That incident was supposedly the origin of the curious ritual, now discontinued, in which newly admitted freemen of the town were required to wade through the deepish water of a local pond.

Alnwick is still an attractive market town, popular with tourists and known among the sporting fraternity as the headquarters of a famous maker of fishing tackle, Hardy Bros. The golf course at Alnmouth a few miles down river is said to be one of the oldest in England, and more recently the little port has become a popular yachting base.

Most of Alnwick's visitors probably come to see the castle, which stands on a mound to the north of the town—a magnificent sight, covering about five acres. It was originally founded about 1140, when a shell keep was constructed around the existing tower, then wooden, and curtain walls replaced the timber palisade of the double bailey. Towers, a powerful gatehouse and barbican were added in the fourteenth century.

Something of the plan and appearance of the medieval castle, the greatest of English border strongholds, can still be seen. But almost nothing is as it was. The castle led a lively existence in its days of greatness, both as military base— William the Lion was captured during a siege in 1174—and as social centre, for the Percies sometimes entertained on a grand scale, but it fell into ruins in the seventeenth century. In the eighteenth century it was turned into a magnificent Gothic mansion for the 1st Duke of Northumberland by Robert Adam, and in the nineteenth century another major reconstruction was effected by Anthony Salvin, when the present Prudhoe Tower and the grand Victorian chambers were created. There is a fine library and collections of good furniture, porcelain, and paintings.

Opposite: It is appropriate that Alnwick Castle, the seat of the dukes of Northumberland, decorates this map of the county produced by Thomas Moule in the 1830s. The dukedom, created in 1766, is younger than the original castle by several centuries.

Below: A view of Alnwick Castle from the East. Note the stone 'defenders' upon the battlements, designed to give an impression of manning.

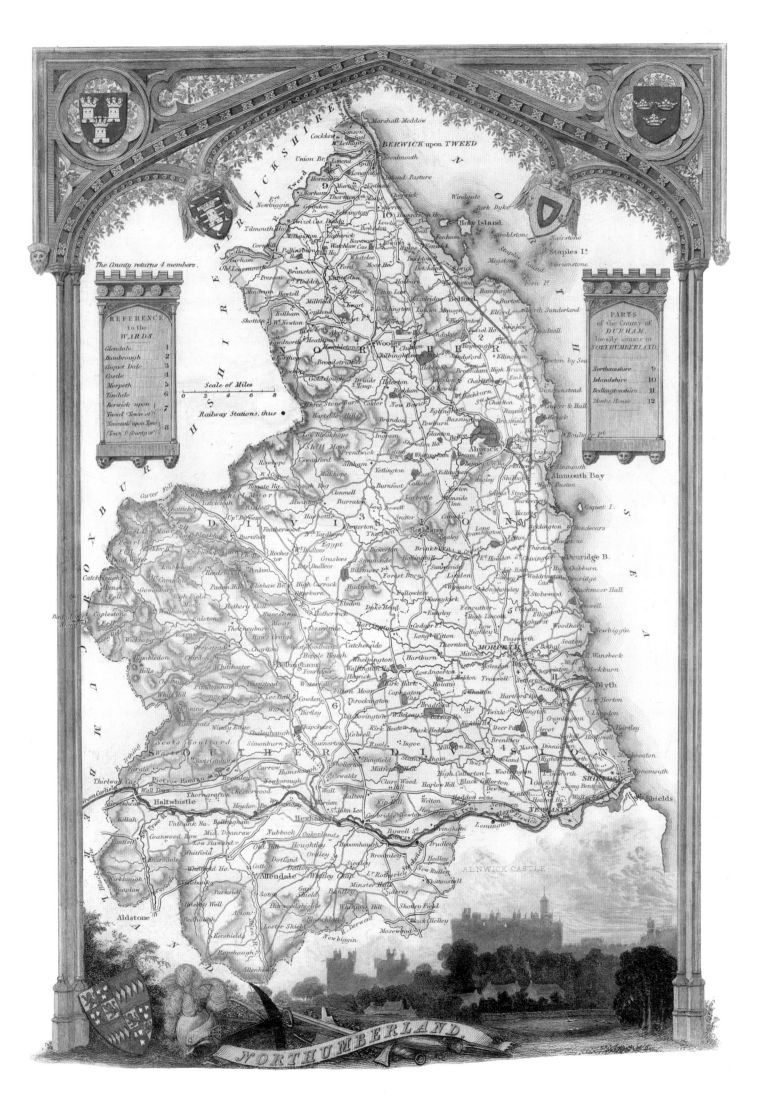

NORTHUMBERLAND.

ARUNDEL

Arundel is a small, affluent town near the Sussex coast. In the Middle Ages, when the sea was closer, it was a substantial port, and it was later linked with London by canal. It is built on a fairly steep slope above the River Arun, with the castle at the top, guarding the gap in the downs created by the river valley. This crucial site was fortified in Saxon times, and the first stone castle was one of the earliest in England.

Since the marriage of the 4th Duke of Norfolk to an heiress of the Fitzalan Family (earls of Arundel) in the sixteenth century, this has been the home of the Howard family, dukes of Norfolk and traditional holders of the office of Earl Marshal. The 16th Duke organized the last royal coronation, even though the Howards are a Roman Catholic family. At Arundel, the Protestant parish church (thirteenth century) is divided by a glass screen, the chancel being the Catholic chapel of the Fitzalans. There is also a nineteenth-century Roman Catholic cathedral in the town, built by the 15th Duke. Indeed, much of Arundel, despite documentary mention of the town as early as the ninth century, is due directly or indirectly to its nineteenth-century landlords. The town hall was provided by the duke and the spacious coaching inn, one of a number of attractive eighteenth-century survivals, is as one might expect named the Norfolk Arms.

Like Windsor, Arundel appears at first glance as a palatial Norman castle and, again like Windsor, it owes that appearance very largely to recent reconstruction. It was built originally by Roger Montgomery, 1st Earl of Arundel, who had it from the Conqueror. To a central round tower, he added curtain walls and the gatehouse known as Earl Roger's Tower. King Henry II took it back after a siege in 1102 and it passed through various hands until it was inherited by John Fitzalan in 1243. After the death of Sir Philip Howard, disinherited by act of attainder in 1572, Arundel passed again to the Crown, but was restored to the Howards by James I. During the Civil War it was besieged and badly knocked about by Sir William Waller: marks on the barbican towers today are said to have been made by the Parliamentary artillery. It was restored as a baronial residence in the eighteenth century (the library remains of that period) and extensively rebuilt in its present form by the 15th Duke between 1890–1903.

Opposite: Originally an eleventh-century motte-and-bailey castle, Arundel was almost completely rebuilt in the eighteenth and nineteenth centuries by its owners, the dukes of Norfolk.

Below: An attractive nineteenth-century map of Sussex by Thomas Moule showing some of the main features of the county, including Arundel Castle.

BAMBURGH

Bamburgh Castle is an imposing sight approached by sea from the Holy Island of Lindisfarne (it can also be seen in the far distance from the Edinburgh–London railway line, weather permitting). It is built on a natural defensive site, on a promontory 150 feet above the sandy beach, with almost vertical cliffs on three sides; the only approach is from the south-east. Film-makers love the place.

This was the chief stronghold of the ancient kings of Northumbria, and it was fortified even earlier, in the sixth century, though there is naturally no evidence of that today. Nor is there much to see of the original Norman castle, often altered since it was built by Roger de Mowbray, Earl of Northumberland in, or very soon after, the Conqueror's time. In the next reign, Bamburgh was besieged by the king, who had another castle built to oppose it which he called 'Malveisin' (Malvoisin) or Evil Neighbour. Though the top storey, at least, was added later, the massive stone tower or keep may have been begun before 1150, when Bamburgh was held for a time by Henry of Huntingdon on behalf of his father, David I, King of Scots. Regained by Henry II, it remained a royal castle thereafter.

The town of Bamburgh, which also possesses a fine thirteenth-century church, grew up around the castle and shared its fortunes, so that it was a much greater place in the Middle Ages than in modern times. Not, however, more peaceful. The inhabitants more than once applied for a remission of taxes 'on account of the robberies and fires inflicted on them by the Scots'. During the Wars of the

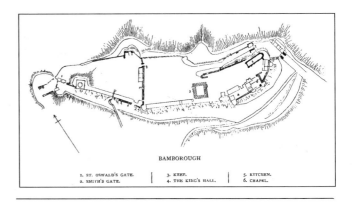

BAMBOROUGH

1. ST. OSWALD'S GATE.   3. KEEP.   5. KITCHEN.
2. SMITH'S GATE.   4. THE KING'S HALL.   6. CHAPEL.

Above: Ground plan of Bamburgh Castle showing its impregnable position on a steeply-cliffed promontory.

Opposite: This dramatic eighteenth-century engraving explains why Iron Age warriors, the Romans, Anglo-Saxons and Vikings all built fortifications on the site where Bamburgh Castle now stands.

Roses, when the castle changed hands four times, it was practically ruined, and dwindled into an unpretentious village, today rather attractive.

The castle itself remained more or less in ruins until the eighteenth century, when Archdeacon Sharp, though only the trustee, put a lot of his own money into its restoration. However, the main restoration work was undertaken, at great expense, at the end of the nineteenth century, after Bamburgh had been bought by the newly ennobled Lord Armstrong, the Newcastle-born inventor and engineer, maker of the Armstrong gun. He bears the chief credit for the awe-inspiring impression the castle makes today.

Barnard Castle

Barnard Castle, attractively situated on the Durham bank of the Tees, is a true castle town. There seems to have been nothing much here before the Norman castle, and the town still bears the castle's name, which derives from its first builder, Bernard (or Barnard) de Baliol. There are other medieval survivals, together with an attractive, octagonal town hall of the mid-eighteenth century and a remarkable museum and art gallery in Bowes Mansion. The town has literary associations too. Rokeby, subject of a poem by Scott, is close by, and a Clockmaker's shop that once stood opposite the King's Head is said to have influenced Dickens in choosing the title *Master Humphrey's Clock* for his weekly magazine. He was staying here, together with his illustrator 'Phiz' (Hablot K. Browne), while researching Yorkshire boarding schools for Nicholas Nickleby in 1838.

Once, the castle was enormous, covering about six acres, and it is unusual in having four wards or baileys, though the so-called Middle Ward is not much more than a small backyard. Little of the castle is left today except the thirteenth-century round tower and some of the walls. The tower, which is almost as wide as it is high (forty feet), is known as the Baliol Tower, after its founders and long-time proprietors. One Baliol founded the college in Oxford (it acquired an extra L—Balliol); his son was briefly King of Scots. The latter, however, not only failed to hang on to the Scottish crown, he was relieved of all his English estates, including Barnard Castle, by Edward I in 1296. Thereafter, possession of the castle was disputed between various proprietors, including the bishops of Durham and the kings of England. The future Richard III, when Earl of Gloucester, gained it as a result of

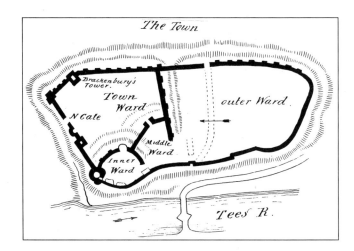

his marriage to Anne Nevill, and his boar's crest may still be seen on a building south of the round tower. The castle was held for Queen Elizabeth against the rebellious northern earls of 1569, but the citizens favoured the rebels, some of the garrison deserted and, after the walls had been breached, Sir George Bowes, the royal steward, was forced to surrender. In the seventeenth century the castle was largely dismantled for the sake of building materials. The last private owner handed over the ruins to the state, then represented by the Ministry of Works, in 1952.

Above: Ground plan of Barnard Castle which clearly shows the layout of the four wards – an unusual feature.

Opposite: The calm achieved in this engraving of the ruins of Barnard Castle belies its stormy history.

Below: An atmospheric engraving illustrating Barnard Castle's imposing situation overlooking the River Tees.

BEAUMARIS

Le beau marais, 'the beautiful marsh', and so it is. The town, the county town of Anglesey though scarcely more than a village, is a charming place, with a fine thirteenth-century church, a superb inn and many houses of similar or slightly later date, as well as a delightful court house of early seventeenth-century origin which has been restored with care and consideration. The nineteenth-century terraces were designed by the prolific Joseph Aloysius Hansom, the designer of a 'patent safety cab' from which the cabs of late Victorian London were descended. The town takes its name from the castle, though it was there first. It was previously called Barnover.

The castle, to the east of the town, guards the eastern end of the Menai Strait, the western end of which is guarded by Caernarvon (p 34) on the mainland. Beaumaris was the last of Edward I's Welsh castles, and was never entirely finished, hence the truncated towers. Despite that it is, if such a word can be applied to so mighty a building, a gem. Because of the level ground, Edward's famous architect, James of St George, was able to devise a symmetrical plan unaffected by geological idiosyncracies. It is a concentric castle with double walls. The outer curtain, which follows the form of a subtle octagon, is reinforced by twelve round towers, and is lower than the inner walls to enable defenders to fire over the top.

Beyond the outer walls was a moat, fed from the sea; ships could anchor in a defended dock under the walls. The inner walls, which are up to sixteen feet thick, surround a bailey which is almost a perfect square. Round towers were stationed at each corner, with two central gatehouses being incomplete. As in other castles of this period, there was no central tower or keep. The two double towered gatehouses were the most substantial single buildings, and contained spacious apartments.

Construction of the castle was notoriously expensive. It is said to have taken thirty-five years to build, but never finished, and at one time to have employed the labour of 3,500 people. Though it capitulated to a siege at the end of the Civil War, this fine example of medieval military engineering was never otherwise attacked.

Opposite: John Speed's map of Anglesey (1610–11) shows how Edward I ensured control of the Menai Straits by situating Beaumaris Castle at one end and Caernarvon Castle at the other. The inset town plan of Beaumaris illustrates the true magnificence of the castle despite its unfinished state.

Below: An engraving by Dove (1774) clearly shows that building work stopped at Beaumaris before the towers were properly finished.

BEAUMARIS

A The Castle
B Castell Street
C Wood Street
D water side
E vtall dore
F Rotten Row
G clyps lane
H Fre schole
I Midele Midge
K Rotten mill
L Rotten Hill
M The Friery

THE SCALE OF FAIRES

CAERNARVON SHYRE

PORT OF BARNS

THE SCALE OF ENGLISH MILES

THE IRISH SEA

MON

TWRKELYN HUNDRED

TALYBOLLION HUNDRED

MENEY HUNDR

TYNDAYTHWY HUND

MALLTRAETH HUNDR

LLYFON HUNDRED

ANGLESEY
Antiently called MONA. Described 1610

NORTH

EAST

SOUTH

WEST

THE OVERGODIAN SEA

Performed by John Speed, and are to be sold in
Popes head alley by John Sudbury and George
Humbolt.
Cum Privilegio.

Iodocus Hondius Calavit
Anno Domini 1613

BELVOIR

Probably the best-known product of Belvoir is the foxhound of that name, distinguished by its dark colouring, which was bred there in the eighteenth century. One of the contributors to its success was the Marquis of Granby, the first Master of Foxhounds to lead a cavalry charge, who is commemorated today on so many inn signs. The famous hunt was founded in 1730 by a group of local gentry, but was soon taken over by the Manners family, dukes of Rutland and proprietors of Belvoir (pronounced 'beever' to confuse the uninitiated) since the fifteenth century. From the terrace of the castle, which dominates the village from its position on a wooded hill, the Leicestershire countryside stretches away to the horizon, all lush green fields, woods and hedges.

The castle today is an unashamed piece of early nineteenth-century Gothic fantasy, with little pretence to be otherwise, but its history goes back to the post-Conquest era, when the first castle was built by a Norman courtier, Robert de Todeni. The medieval structure survived until the Wars of the Roses, but was subsequently largely dismantled by Lord Hastings in order to rebuild the castle at Ashby-de-la-Zouche, which he had acquired in the wake of the dynastic conflict. Belvoir Castle was rebuilt by the 1st Earl of Rutland early in the sixteenth century, but dismantled again by order of Parliament after the seventeenth-century Civil War.

It was again rebuilt, in more domestic style, by the 8th Earl, and this third version housed his descendants until, in 1800, the 5th Duke decided that something fancier was called for. He hired James Wyatt, who was assisted by the duke's chaplain, Revd. Sir John Thoroton, a man of high-flown architectural ideas. Since Wyatt died in 1813 and the new building was devastated by fire in 1816, it is uncertain how much is due to Wyatt, though his sons were responsible for the magnificent state apartments, including the French Rococo Elizabeth Salon, named after the duchess, herself something of a connoisseur. There are paintings by Holbein, Poussin and Gainsborough among other art treasures.

Old traditions are maintained, but things are not quite the same as they were when the guest list included the Prince Regent, the Duke of Wellington and Beau Brummel.

Opposite: The battlements of Belvoir are all too obviously the product of Gothic fantasy. The castle's appearance is largely the result of work ordered to be done by the 5th Duchess of Rutland in the early nineteenth century.

Below: A lavishly illustrated map by Thomas Moule shows Belvoir Castle and the famous foxhounds which were bred by the dukes of Rutland during the eighteenth century.

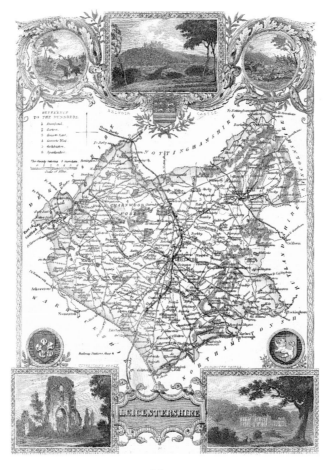

BERKELEY

The town of Berkeley lies in the Vale of Berkeley, east of the River Severn and west of the Cotswolds. Much of this land is low-lying, flat and watery—there is a famous haven for waterfowl five miles upstream at Slimbridge—but the town occupies a slight rise. A recent guidebook remarks that the liveliest noise in Berkeley comes from the kennels of the fox hounds. Traffic, others would say, runs them close.

Perhaps the most remarkable thing about Berkeley Castle is that it has been constantly occupied by the same family since the twelfth century. Though great warriors, the Berkeleys fortunately never rose to the top ranks of the feudal pyramid, and thus did not acquire powerful enemies to deprive them of their inheritance. The family's ancestor was Robert Fitzharding, who was granted the manor of Berkeley about 1150, his successors describing themselves as 'of Berkeley', hence the surname. The king apparently assisted in reconstruction of the castle, then no doubt wooden. A shell keep about sixty feet high was built, with a curtain wall enclosing the bailey, and various other buildings within.

The most notorious event in the history of the castle took place in 1327, when King Edward II was murdered there on the orders of the queen and her lover, Roger Mortimer. The Berkeleys can disclaim responsibility: Lord Berkeley had been relieved as the king's keeper because he was too lenient. That was certainly not a fault of his replacements, who killed the king with notorious savagery.

A room in a turret of the shell keep is preserved, it is said, as it was when Edward was killed there. Yet the castle was almost entirely rebuilt a few years later. The magnificent

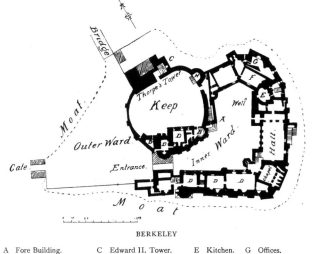

BERKELEY

A Fore Building. C Edward II. Tower. E Kitchen. G Offices.
B Edward II. Dungeon. D Domestic Apartments. F Buttery. H Oratory and Well.

great hall, with saddle-beam timber roof and distinctive arches, dates from that time. The Anglo-Norman shell keep, displaying damage from the Civil War, and outer walls in red sandstone remain. Later alterations have enhanced the building. Early in this century the 8th Earl of Berkeley embarked on a fruitful quest in France, returning with furniture, stone fireplaces and carved doors, such as that in the—modern—clock tower.

Above: Ground plan of Berkeley, a typical motte castle, built shortly after the Norman Conquest. The motte (mound) was an essential feature of Norman castles.

Opposite: The original motte castle at Berkeley was given to the Fitzhardings by Henry II. The family, whose descendants still own the castle, made substantial alterations to it over the centuries changing its appearance almost beyond recognition.

BODIAM

The medieval manor of Bodiam, on the River Rother where East Sussex borders on Kent, was situated at a point where the river was navigable down to the sea. In the late fourteenth century, this seemed more of a drawback than an advantage. The French held temporary command of the Channel, and in 1377 they launched raids on Rye, at the mouth of the Rother, and other places on the south coast. There was not much to stop them sailing up the river, and in 1385 Sir Edward Dalyngrigge had no difficulty in gaining a royal licence to fortify and add battlements to his manor house at Bodiam.

Sir Edward in fact abandoned the old manor in favour of an entirely new building, one of the last and finest, seriously intended medieval castles in England. The plan is simple: curtain walls with sixty-foot round towers at the four corners surround an almost-square bailey. The longer walls each have a central, square tower attached, and the other two walls have centred gatehouses. The northern one is a formidable structure of two rectilinear towers with a deep arch guarded by three portcullises (one capable of being shut against the interior, an unusual precaution against a fifth column). This was the main element of the castle. The building is in the middle of an artificial lake, which is fed from the Rother. Now the castle is reached by a simple causeway; Sir Edward Dalyngrigge, needless to say, constructed a much more devious approach involving a barbican, the remains of which were discovered when the lake was drained during the early part of this century.

As things turned out, Bodiam Castle proved an unnecessary precaution. Within a few years, Henry V was on the throne, and the French were in no position to contemplate cross-Channel raids. The castle's history has been fairly tranquil. It was twice briefly subjected to siege, capitulating quickly when threatened with Parliamentary cannon in the Civil War, and it gradually mouldered away until Lord Curzon, ex-Viceroy of India, bought it in 1917 and restored the walls and towers to their medieval appearance. The interiour buildings have all gone, though we can surmise that Sir Edward did not neglect comfort nor convenience (there were twenty-eight lavatories discharging into the lake). What remains is an empty shell. Nevertheless, Bodiam is a romantic sight, and if any castle can be called 'pretty', this must be the prettiest castle in England.

Opposite: The idyllic setting of Bodiam Castle makes it one of England's most beautiful castles. It was stylishly restored by Lord Curzon in 1920.

Below: A ground-floor plan of Bodiam Castle shows the fortified towers in the corners of the quadrangle, and the square interval towers in the east and west walls.

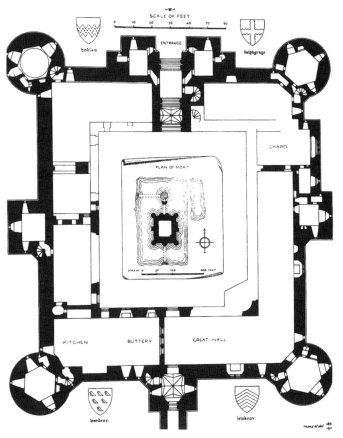

BROUGH

The ruins of Brough Castle occupy a lofty site in the Vale of Eden, overlooking Swindale Beck and commanding a crossing of the Pennines, on the main road between Appleby and Barnard Castle (p 18). The strategic importance of the site was first exploited by the Romans, who built a substantial fort, Verterae, here. When William Rufus came to construct a royal castle, parts of the Roman building were incorporated. Some Roman earthworks are still visible, and there is a stretch of Norman work in the north wall; otherwise, nothing remains of these early fortifications. The Norman castle was destroyed by William the Lion, King of Scotland, during his invasion of 1174, was rebuilt and, early in the thirteenth century, came into the possession of the formidable Clifford family. The Scots attacked it again in 1314 after Bannockburn, where the 1st Lord Clifford was killed, but, while the village of Brough was burned down, the castle itself apparently suffered only superficial damage. The 2nd Lord Clifford was hanged as a rebel in 1322, but the family regained the estates and also survived the career of the 9th Baron, who earned the nickname 'Butcher' for his activities during the Wars of the Roses and was killed fighting for the Lancastrians in 1461.

Complaints about the condition of the castle had been made at various times, though remarks about 'disrepair' and even 'ruin' may have meant little more than that it was not in an acceptable state for a royal visit. However, in 1521 the interior was entirely gutted by fire, and the castle remained derelict until the seventeenth century, when it was restored by that notable builder, Lady Anne Clifford, Countess Dowager of Pembroke (1590–1676). She also restored other Clifford castles, including Skipton (p 106), not to mention the church in nearby Appleby, where she is buried. Another fire destroyed part of her work, and after her death the castle again fell rapidly into decline, its stones carried off for building elsewhere. After part of what remained of the great tower, or keep, fell down in 1920, its current owner surrendered it to the state. Besides the remains of this building, parts of which date from the twelfth century, the most substantial survival is the round tower known as Clifford's Tower. This too is of twelfth- or thirteenth-century origin, but is mainly the work of Lady Anne. Sheep still graze on the sward below the impressive ruins of the keep.

Opposite: Brough was sited to afford control of the upper reaches of Edendale, where the old Roman road begins its long climb over Stainmoor to the east.

Below: Thomas Moule's map of Westmoreland (now part of Cumbria) shows Brough Castle after it was restored by Anne, Countess Dowager of Dorset, Pembroke and Montgomery.

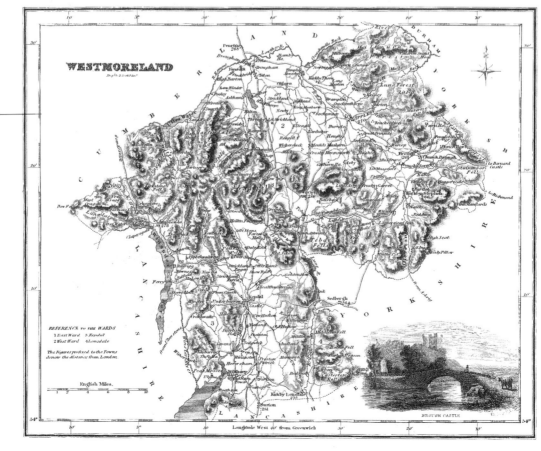

CAERLAVEROCK

The ruined castle of Caerlaverock stands in marshy fields close to the Solway Firth, at the foot of Nithsdale, about eight miles south of Dumfries. Remains of a Roman fort have been found a mile or two to the north. Caerlaverock was for centuries a stronghold of a famous Border clan, the Maxwells, later earls of Nithsdale. The first of the Maxwells who held the castle was probably John Maccuswell, Chamberlain of Scotland, who died in 1241. The present castle, however, dates from about 1290. There is some doubt surrounding its origins, partly because of its unusual shape, suggesting an architect with novel ideas. The plan of the castle is a simple triangle, with round towers at two angles and a great double-towered gatehouse at the third, facing north. Though the castle is ruined, the towers, rebuilt with added machicolation in the fifteenth century, and gun ports inserted in the sixteenth, still stand.

Although the castle changed hands several times in the course of the Scottish Wars of Independence, and the English held it for twelve years following a successful siege by Edward I, its defences were formidable. Outside the walls lay a moat, beyond that earthworks, no doubt also a palisade, and a second moat with further earthworks—they may be seen extending deep into Castle Wood—beyond that. Having been recaptured by forces loyal to the Bruce, the castle was dismantled to prevent the English using it again, but subsequently rebuilt on the original plan. The Maxwells were at the height of their power in the fifteenth century, after the collapse of the Black Douglases, but apart from Border raids they were involved in an endless feud with the Johnstones. The 6th Lord Maxwell was killed by the Johnstones in a battle at Lockerbie in 1593, but Border warfare was coming to an end and the 8th Lord Maxwell (1st Earl of Nithsdale) felt able to introduce a more domestic note at Caerlaverock by building a kind of Renaissance villa within the walls. The defences were maintained, nevertheless, and in 1640 the castle was held against the Covenanters during a three-month siege. Though not surrendered, it sustained severe damage, and this time it was not repaired.

Opposite: The three-storey residential block at Caerlaverock Castle was a seventeenth-century addition by Lord Nithsdale. Its style clashes with the rest of the medieval building.

Below: The formidable gatehouse of the unique, triangular-plan castle of Caerlaverock that stands on the northern shore of the Solway Firth.

CAERNARVON

Of Edward I's four main Welsh castles, Beaumaris (p 22) is the most aesthetically satisfying, Harlech (p 76) the most picturesque and Conwy (p 54) the most intimidating. Nevertheless, Caernarvon is easily the grandest. It was intended from the beginning to be the seat of English royal government in Wales, and the polygonal towers may have been designed to add a touch of distinction absent from Edward's other Welsh castles. He may have been influenced by the magnificent architecture of Constantinople, where he would have spent time during the Crusades.

The castle is unusual in plan, taking the form of an irregular figure eight. The residential quarters were located in the thirteen massive towers (no two alike). The chief of these was the Eagle Tower, named after the stone eagles that surmounted its turrets. This would have been occupied by the royal governor, or justiciar, of North Wales, and was capable of providing suitably roomy living space since, despite the girth of the walls, the internal diameter is about forty feet. Visitors of high rank may have arrived by water and entered the castle via the water gate in the Eagle Tower.

Caernarvon Castle was built on a flat spit of land projecting into the Menai Strait. For centuries it was bordered by water on three sides, but the little River Cadnant, which flowed into the Seiont east of the castle, has since been built over. The medieval town, on the north side, was entirely enclosed by walls extending from the castle, which still stand. This close association of townsfolk with castle was no doubt intended to keep at least some Welsh people loyal. The street plan has not changed since the Middle Ages, but a view of the town about 1750 shows that houses had already been built beyond the walls.

Caernarvon was first fortified by a Norman earl of Chester about 1100, although the remains may still be seen of a Roman fort on rising ground beyond the medieval town. Like King Edward later, both the Romans and the Welsh princes administered North Wales from Caernarvon, which was the scene of many episodes in Welsh resistance to English rule. In 1282 King Edward I brought off a propaganda coup by presenting the Welsh with a prince who was 'born in Wales and spoke no English'. The prince was his newly born son, the future Edward II, who naturally spoke neither English nor any other language. (He could not have been born in the Eagle Tower, as legend maintains, because the castle had only been founded a matter of months previously). An echo of these events occurred in 1969 when the Queen formally invested her eldest son as Prince of Wales.

Opposite: Caernarvon was intended to be the special symbol of Edward I's sovereignty over Wales. This engraving is fine evidence that this aim was brilliantly realized.

Below: W. H. Bartlett's engraving (1840) captures the might of Caernarvon Castle – the keystone of Edward I's military strategy for the conquest of north Wales.

CAERPHILLY

Almost every castle has something unique about it, but Caerphilly is outstanding in several ways. It is, for a start, the largest castle in Wales, or even in Britain if government headquarters and royal palaces are excluded. It is also of great architectural interest. Though not the first concentric castle—i.e. one with two curtain walls with an outer bailey in between—in Britain, it is the first to be built as such more or less from scratch. Caerphilly also illustrates the argument that, if you can't build your castle on a convenient hill, then you might do worse than build it in a valley since valleys can be flooded. Finally, the castle has survived the centuries with remarkably little damage, aided by sensitive restoration. The town of Caerphilly grew up around the castle. Its chief claim to fame otherwise was the manufacture of Caerphilly cheese. Cheese is no longer made there, nor is coal mined in the valley.

The builder of Caerphilly Castle was Gilbert de Clare, an important lord of the Marches, and it was begun in 1271, thus predating the great Welsh castles of Edward I. Indeed its main purpose was as a weapon against Llwelyn, Prince of Wales, who flattened an earlier attempt to build it in 1268.

The outer bailey is surrounded by a relatively low curtain wall, with two gatehouses and a water gate handily placed for the kitchen. The main stronghold is a rectangular enclosure with immense round towers at the corners and gatehouses in the east and west: all of these elements are virtually independent forts. Most of this was built within ten years of the castle's foundation, and nearly all of it is in place today. The north-east tower is ruined, and the south-east tower is split from top to bottom and famously tilting. Some say the tilt dates from a medieval siege, others say Civil War mining was responsible, though one takes off one's hat to any sappers who got near enough. For—another extraordinary feature—the castle has extensive water defences which include a mighty, 1,000-foot barrage, serving both as a dam and as an extra defencework. It is difficult to appreciate the size and sophistication of this system except from the air. Altogether, this is a breathtaking place, often described as one of the finest surviving examples of military architecture to be seen anywhere in Europe.

Opposite: South-west view of Caerphilly Castle. Built towards the end of the thirteenth century, it stood as one of the finest examples of military architecture in Europe.

Below: The general plan of Caerphilly Castle shows the concentric main castle block with its two twin-towered gatehouses in the west and east walls.

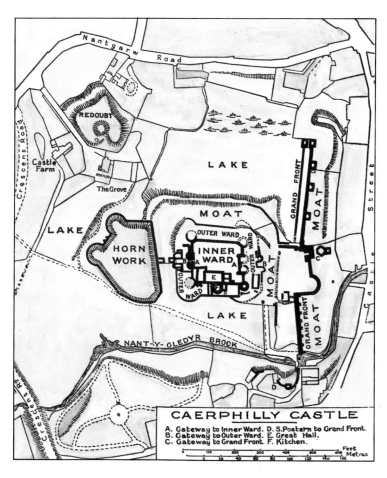

CAERPHILLY CASTLE

A. Gateway to Inner Ward. D. S. Postern to Grand Front.
B. Gateway to Outer Ward. E. Great Hall.
C. Gateway to Grand Front. F. Kitchen.

CARISBROOKE

Carisbrooke was once the capital of the Isle of Wight, though it was never much larger than the village that exists today. It is dominated by the Norman castle from whose ramparts there is a magnificent view over the countryside. The church, with a fine Perpendicular tower, is all that remains of a Cistercian abbey, and there are remains of a Roman villa, but the village itself, though it had a market, never amounted to much except through its association with the government and the seat of the lord of the Isle of Wight. From the late thirteenth century this was a royal official— the last governor was a daughter of Queen Victoria.

The Anglo-Norman structure was a motte castle, originally earth and rubble but apparently stone by 1136, when an irregular shell keep was constructed around it. The adjoining bailey was then given curtain walls with flanking square towers. Extensive additions were made in the thirteenth to fourteenth centuries, including the dominant feature, a twin-towered gatehouse, with parapet and machiolations (holes in the floor for dropping nasty objects—perhaps boiling oil even—on attackers). A feature of the castle that always fascinates visitors is the well, said to be over 160 feet deep.

There were further large-scale alterations under Elizabeth I, designed to make the castle better able to resist likely attack by Spanish artillery. An Italian engineer built extensive earthworks, and some additions were made to the residential buildings in the bailey in the same period. The Spaniards failed to effect their landing in 1588, and apart from a siege during the Stephen-Matilda wars and one unsuccessful assault by the French in the reign of Richard II, Carisbrooke Castle has seen less trouble than might have been expected in the course of eight centuries. It is commonly associated with King Charles I who, trying to make a dash for the Channel Islands after breaking off talks with the army at Hampton Court in 1647, was imprisoned at Carisbrooke for over a year. His son Henry and daughter Elizabeth (Charles I had nine children) were also brought here as prisoners after their father's execution; Princess Elizabeth died at Carisbrooke. The chapel was restored at the beginning of this century as a memorial to King Charles.

Opposite: Carisbrooke Castle, seen here as a decorative feature of a map of the Isle of Wight by Thomas Moule, was the largest and strongest of all the fortresses on the island.

Below: The twin-turreted gatehouse of Carisbrooke Castle was built around 1335 and has grooves for three portcullises.

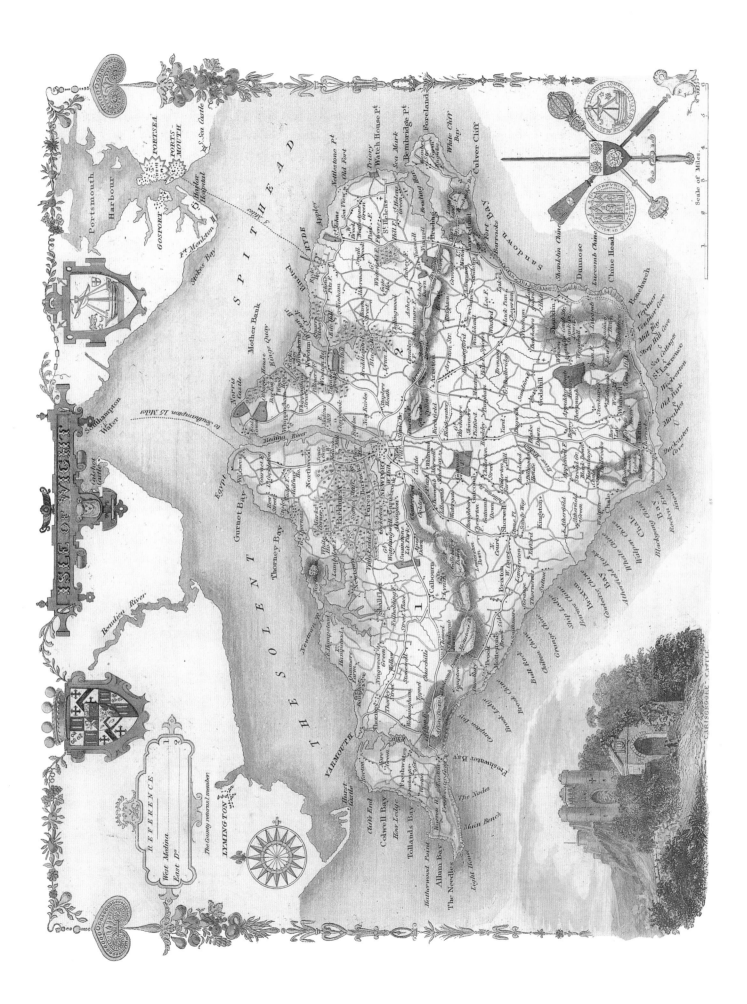

ISLE OF WIGHT

Portsmouth Harbour

PORTSEA
PORTS-
MOUTH
L. Sea Castle

GOSPORT
Ft Monkston
Military Hospital

Stokes Bay

Southampton Water

SPITHEAD

Mother Bank

to Southampton 15 Miles

Beaulieu River

Norris Castle
Cowes

Egypt

Medina River

Gurnet Bay

THE SOLENT

Thorney Bay

Calshot Castle

REFERENCE.
West Medina
East Do
The County returns 1 member.

LYMINGTON

Yarmouth

Hurst Castle
Cliff End
Colwell Bay
How Ledge
Tallands Bay
Hatherwood Point
Alum Bay
The Needles
Light House

Freshwater Bay
The Nodes
Main Bench

RYDE
Binstead

St Helens
Sea View
Priory
Nettlestone Pt
Watch House Pt
Sea Mark
Dembridge Pt
Foreland

White Cliff Bay
Culver Cliff

Sandown Bay

Shanklin Chine
Dunnose
Luccomb Chine
Chine Head

Bonchurch
Ventnor
Mill Bay
Steep Hill Cove
St Lawrence
Wolverton
Old Park
Mirables
Buckaster Cove

Blackgang Chine
Whale Chine
Atherfield Ledge
Brook Chine
Cowleaze Chine
Grange Chine

NEWPORT
Carisbrook
Parkhurst Forest
Northwood

FRESHWATER BAY

CARISBROOK CASTLE

CARLISLE

Considering its history of violence and devastation, Carlisle is an impressive, even grand, city today. Its prosperity, however, dates from fairly recent times. The castle was last besieged in 1746, and for many centuries before that Carlisle was an unpromising place to do business. It lies less than ten miles from the Scottish border, where the Caldew and the Petteril join the River Eden not far from its mouth on the Solway Firth. The Romans were here in strength: evidence of their presence frequently appears whenever the soil is turned over. The original fort developed into a town of some size, Luguvallium, where a fountain was still evident when St Cuthbert came here in 686. Later, stone from the town and the fort by Hadrian's Wall was used in the construction of the castle. The town was destroyed by the Danes in the ninth century and for a time all but abandoned. At that time Carlisle, inasmuch as it belonged to anyone, was Scottish, but towards the end of the eleventh century William Rufus claimed it and built the first—no doubt wooden—castle.

For the next seven centuries Carlisle was embroiled in Anglo-Scottish contests. King David II of Scots took it in 1135, and later died there, but Henry II of England regained it in 1157, and from that time it remained English, though not peacefully so. Both monarchs were responsible for some construction of the castle, though it is uncertain who did what. Carlisle's history of conflict meant that the castle underwent frequent physical changes: part of it, including the hall where Edward I held several parliaments, was demolished as late as the nineteenth century, when the building that houses the museum of the Border Regiment was constructed. The most impressive building now is the tower or keep, which dates back to the twelfth century, though most of the fabric has been renewed at various later times. The fourteenth-century gatehouse also survives. Queen Mary's Tower commemorates the visit of Mary Queen of Scots, who stayed here on what proved to be her fatal journey to England in 1568.

The accession of James VI to the English throne in 1603 signalled an end to Border raids, but not to rough times for Carlisle. The castle was twice besieged in the Civil War, when part of the cathedral was pulled down in order to repair the castle, and severely battered again a century later when briefly held for Prince Charles Edward.

Opposite: The massive tower that dominates Carlisle Castle was built some time between 1136 and 1174. The original medieval castle was transformed by Henry VIII into a powerful gun-fort.

Below: Speed's map of Cumberland contains an attractive detail of Carlisle showing the castle sitting within the city walls. The walls were first built on the orders of Henry I in 1122, thirty years after William Rufus had built the first – wooden – castle in the city.

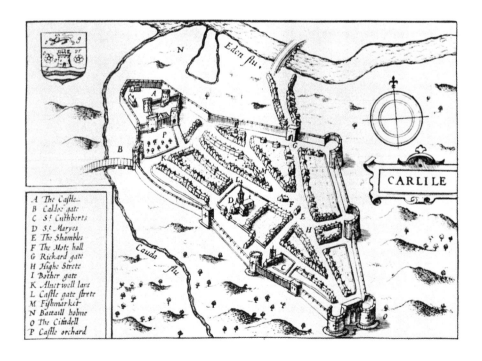

A The Castle
B Caldos gate
C St Cuthberts
D St Maryes
E The Shambles
F The Mote hall
G Rickard gate
H Highe Strete
I Bother gate
K Alnerwell lane
L Castle gate strete
M Fyshmarket
N Battaill holme
O The Citadell
P Castle orchard

CASTLE CAMPBELL

The village of Dollar lies in fine countryside about fourteen miles east of Stirling, and is of architectural interest for two very different reasons. In the nineteenth century it became a famous centre of education thanks to a native benefactor, John McNab, who rose from poverty to become a rich shipowner and endowed the Dollar academy for the education of poor boys like himself. (In the event, the academy's high reputation attracted not-so-poor people from outside the district.) The buildings, completed before 1820, were designed by William Playfair, architect of the Scottish National Gallery, in the Greek Revival style. He was also responsible for the unpretentious houses of Academy Square.

A steep hill close to the town is the source of the two streams that combine to form the burn of Dollar. Their names are Sorrow and Care, and the stronghold that crowns the hill was once known as Gloom Castle. If all this were not sufficiently depressing, the castle contains a pit prison that must conjure up ghastly images in the mind of even the most unimaginative visitor.

Gloom Castle came to the 1st Earl of Argyll in the late fifteenth century as part of his wife's dowry. With customary Campbell acumen, he had picked the right side to support in the quarrel between King James III and his son (James IV). Argyll was a man who 'served his country well, his county better and his clan and family best of all'; among other favours he persuaded the king to sanction the change of name from Gloom Castle to Castle Campbell. It was maintained as a Campbell stronghold until the seventeenth century civil wars, when it was besieged by allies of Montrose and later burned by General Monk; afterwards it was abandoned.

The oldest and most interestesting part of Castle Campbell is the lofty rectangular tower, probably built by the 1st Earl on the site of an earlier motte castle. It has four floors, rising to a parapet over sixty feet high, and is remarkably well preserved, suggesting that its seventeenth-century conquerors did less damage than alleged. The largely ruin buildings around the courtyard are of later date. The view of the Forth valley from the top of the tower is truly spectacular.

Opposite: Castle Campbell occupies one of the most spectacular sites of all British castles, standing on a spur of the Ochil Hills overlooking Dollar Glen and the Firth of Forth.

Below: The ceiling of the top floor of Castle Campbell's tower was vaulted many years after it was built in the fifteenth century.

CASTLE RISING

According to legend, the last missile to strike the walls of Castle Rising was a ball from the nearby cricket ground, struck by a member of Harlequins Rugby Football Club which in the 1950s used to send a cricket team to challenge the village. But it would have been a very long hit; perhaps the tale was improved in retelling in the bar of the Red Cat.

This part of the country was relatively more prosperous in the Middle Ages. Castle Rising is about five miles north of King's Lynn, once an important port, and the village, which then had access to the sea itself, is described in a Victorian gazeteer, rather unkindly, as 'a decayed remnant' of a formerly significant borough. Present visitors, while admiring the seventeenth-century almshouses, would not guess that Castle Rising once had a mayor and corporation, regular fairs and markets, and even—until 1832—an MP, though they might surmise from the fine Norman church and the castle that things are not quite what they used to be.

The manor of Castle Rising, recorded in Domesday Book, was granted to William de Albini in the late eleventh century, and the castle was built about 1140 by his successor, who was Earl of Lincoln and husband of Henry I's widow. In 1332 it was sold to the notorious Queen Isabella, who lived there, maintaining a low profile, after plotting the death of her husband Edward II. It remained a royal castle until Henry VIII bartered it with the Duke of Norfolk. Today it is in the hands of English Heritage.

The chief glory of Castle Rising is the magnificent Norman tower or keep which, thanks partly to the fact that the castle never came under siege, is in a remarkably good state of preservation, retaining plenty of Norman decoration such as bands of interlacing blind arches. Even more interesting, perhaps, since similar examples are so rare, are the earthen

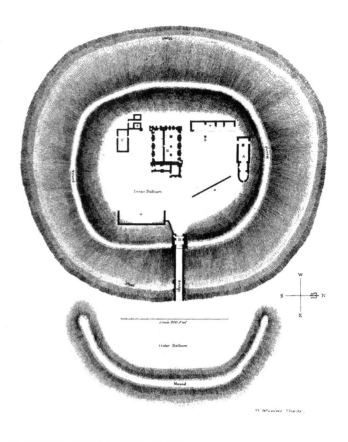

Above: The banks and ditches that surround Castle Rising are among the best examples of Norman defensive earthwork fortifications in Britain.

Opposite: This fine engraving shows the elaborate external ornament that decorates the outer walls of Castle Rising.

defenceworks, which cover an area of about twelve acres. Excavation is still underway here, and various mysteries remain to be solved, though Roman remains have been established. The moat, backed by an immense oval rampart over sixty feet high, is itself about sixty feet deep and may have been deeper. Remains of a rectangular gatehouse have survived to this day and can still be seen.

CAWDOR

A nineteenth-century visitor to this fine old tower house, a few miles south of Nairn, remarked that 'the whole of Cawdor castle is peculiarly calculated to impress the mind with a retrospect of past ages, feudal customs, and deeds of darkness.' Seen on a sunny day with the magnificent gardens in full flower, deeds of darkness spring less easily to mind; nevertheless, legends accrue around the seat of the Campbells of Cawdor, some of them decidedly grisly. It is said, for example, that the mother of the thanes and earls of Cawdor, a much sought-after heiress born shortly after the death of her father, was branded as a baby by her mother (alternatively, had the top joint of a finger bitten off by her nurse) to frustrate any possibility of impersonation.

Within the castle grows an ancient hawthorn, carefully protected in a wire cage. In 1454 the Thane of Calder (Cawdor) resolved to build a new castle. He had a dream (or, possibly, consulted a local seer), telling him he should place a chest of gold on a donkey and let it wander. Where it stopped would be the place to build. It halted at the hawthorn tree, and the tower was built around it. Tests suggest that the hawthorn could be that old (if they had suggested otherwise, no Campbell would have believed them). On the other hand, the Sassenach legend that Macbeth was an early Thane of Cawdor and that King Duncan was done to death on the premises cannot be substantiated. Nevertheless, a room in the tower was, in a more gullible age, shown to visitors as the scene of Duncan's death.

Though not as old as Macbeth, Cawdor Castle is an early tower house and is also one of the few medieval castles in Scotland still privately inhabited. The main residential buildings to the north and east of the tower are largely seventeenth-century. The castle contains some good tapestries and many memorabilia of the Campbells of Cawdor, a race distinguished for their military achievements. The late Sir Iain Moncrieffe of that ilk, a great man for obscure genealogical facts, calculated that the fifty-odd male descendants of the Earl of Cawdor in the past hundred years who were of an age for military service in wartime had between them won twenty-two British awards for bravery, including three Victoria Crosses.

Opposite: The curtain wall that surrounded the tower at Cawdor has been replaced by largely seventeenth-century buildings on the north and east, away from the stream that defends the western approach.

Below: The fortified part of Cawdor Castle was partly built with the masonry from an earlier building on the site which was demolished when Cawdor was planned.

Chepstow

The unusual plan of Chepstow Castle is dictated by the site, a long and narrow ridge above the River Wye. It is an obvious strategic vantage point from which to launch raids into Wales or to intercept Welsh raids into England. Moreover, it marks, approximately, the limit of Wye navigation for all but small boats. There was a Roman ford here, close to the attractive, early nineteenth-century bridge by John Rennie.

Although a settlement existed here from very early times, Chepstow is essentially a fortress town. It had some importance as a port, though goods transhipped there originated in, and were mostly destined for, other places. Chepstow—still essentially medieval, with its steep little streets, its fine, formerly monastic church, and some remnants of the old wall—never seems to have had a market, and there is no record of significant manufacturing. Income was mainly derived from dues levied on ships.

The founder of the castle was the Norman Earl of Hereford, William FitzOsborn. It must have been one of the earliest stone castles in England, begun within two or three years of the Conquest. He erected, or at least started, a rectangular 'keep' two storeys in height which, on the narrow site, almost divided the bailey in two. During the next 200 years or so, Chepstow passed through the hands of a variety of feudal lords, including the Clares and the Bigods, and construction continued: very little of the original Norman building is left. The central keep was heightened and a powerful curtain wall was erected, effectively dividing the eastern bailey into two. A barbican was built to the west, defending the western bailey, and a twin-towered gatehouse in the east. It contained one of those lovely medieval prisons

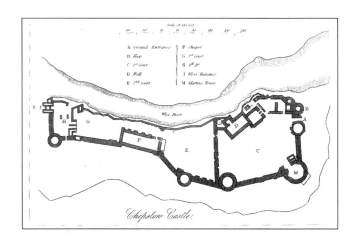

Above: Chepstow Castle was built over several periods. The great tower and chapel (F) were built *c.* 1070. The barbican (H) was built between 1225 and 1245.

Opposite: Henry Marten, one of the men who signed Charles I's death warrant, was held prisoner at Chepstow Castle for twenty years. The tower in which he was incarcerated now bears his name.

Below: Chepstow Castle overlooks the harbour from which it was provisioned by ships sailing up the River Wye from Bristol.

the only access to which is a hole in the roof. The western gatehouse and the massive D-plan tower on the south-east corner, now known as Marten's Tower, were built towards the end of the thirteenth century. Though the castle is ruined. all these features—and more—are evident today, for Chepstow survived the Middle Ages without serious attack, and in spite of being besieged during the Civil War, it suffered little damage. Some minor alterations were made in the late seventeenth century, when it was used as a prison. After two centuries of neglect—glassmaking went on in the ruins—it passed into state care.

CHESTER

Like most old cities, Chester, has been through some troubled times, yet it remains, more than almost any other city in England, remarkably unspoiled. Perhaps the most improbable survival is the city walls, a good part of which are Roman. They run for about two miles, virtually intact.

Deva, as it was then called, was the headquarters of the 20th Legion, responsible for keeping marauding Welsh tribes in check, and the town became a busy port. After the Romans left, it fell into decline and by the tenth century was said to be derelict, but it revived under the Saxon King Athelstan and still more after the Norman Conquest, when it became once more a major centre of commerce and shipbuilding. The Norman earls of Chester built a timber castle where the present one now stands. The stone castle, though incorporating some earlier construction, dates from the reign of Henry III when, after the death of the redoubtable Earl Ranulph, Chester passed to the Crown. The Normans also built a splendid church intended as a cathedral but superseded by Coventry, and during the course of the Middle Ages the familiar galleried shops known as the Rows appeared (though no one knows how or why). Towers and gates were added to the renewed city walls, including the massive Water Tower (1322) and Eastgate, which now spans the street of that name. The city became renowned for its pageants and mystery plays performed in Abbey Square.

From about the fourteenth century, Chester became less prosperous. The bridge was swept away in the flood, the port silted up and trade died off. The Benedictine abbey was dissolved, though its ancient, pre-Norman church remained to become the cathedral of a new diocese, and much of the old monastic buildings survived. These misfortunes apart, the wool trade picked up after the arrival of weavers from Norwich and the clearing of the channel of the Dee. In more recent times Chester has benefited from the many visitors it has attracted.

The castle, which had survived siege in the Civil War with little damage, was partly reconstructed at the end of the eighteenth century, losing its battlements and some of its walls in the process. Within the new buildings then erected is now the regimental museum of the Cheshires.

Opposite: This nineteenth-century map of Chester shows the castle's position on the banks of the River Dee in the south of the city. Charles I stood on the city walls, seen on the lower right of the map, watching his defeated troops return to the city.

Below: Chester Castle was built on the site of a motte castle raised by William the Conqueror in 1069–70, just outside the site of the old Roman town.

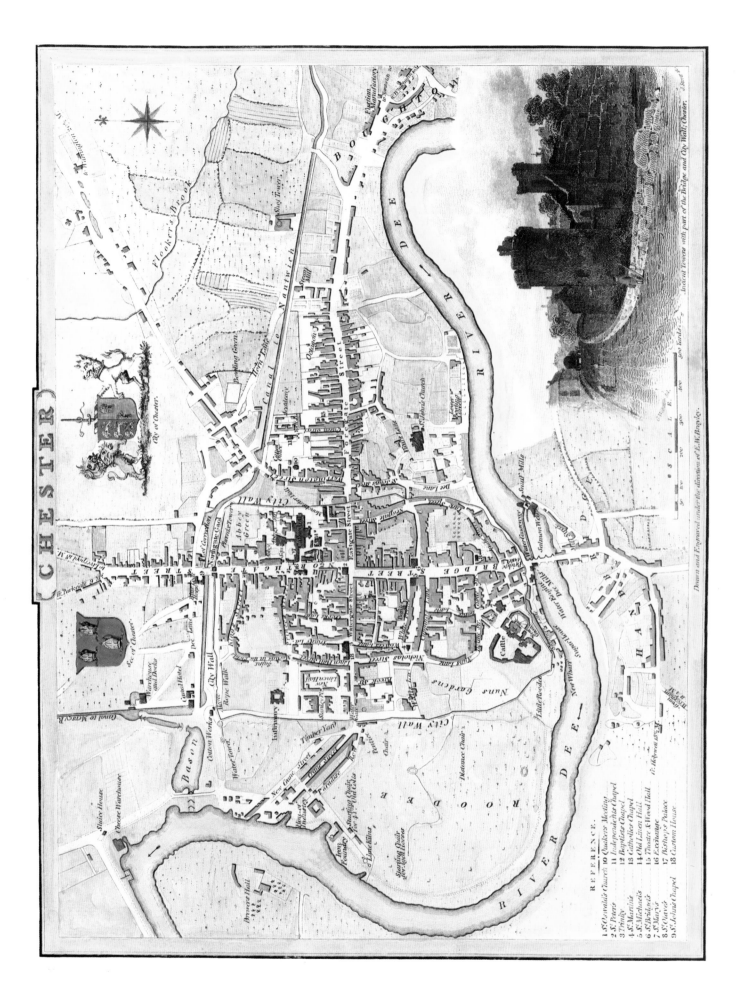

CHESTER

City of Chester

See of Chester

REFERENCE.

1 S.t Oswald's Church 10 Quakers Meeting
2 S.t Peters   11 Independents Chapel
3 Trinity   12 Baptists Chapel
4 S.t Martins   13 Catholics Chapel
5 S.t Michaels   14 Old Linen Hall
6 S.t Brides   15 Theatre & Wood Hall
7 S.t Mary's   16 Exchange
8 S.t Olaves   17 Bishops Palace
9 S.t John's Chapel   18 Custom House

Drawn and Engraved under the direction of E.W. Brayley.

Ancient Towers with part of the Bridge and City Walls, Chester.

RIVER DEE

ROODEE

Nuns Gardens

CONISBROUGH

Conisbrough is a poor Yorkshire mining village, about five miles from Doncaster, the kind of place where the inhabitants used to keep coal in the bath—or so the gentry believed. It is not one of those Yorkshire villages that attract tourists and TV producers, nor does its name resound through the pages of history. Even in these bleak times, there is evidence of Yorkshire grit and humour in the shops and pubs, but visitors to the area can be assumed to be bent on viewing the castle, famous for featuring in Scott's novel *Ivanhoe* and also for the unusual nature of its structure which is unique within England.

The central building is a massive tower, one of the first circular great towers in the country. It is supported by six immense buttresses, like attached towers themselves, which are almost square in plan but slightly tapered to form an outward-directed wedge shape. Originally they were about 100 feet high, slightly outreaching the tower itself. The whole structure stands on a mound and has a markedly splayed plinth, like Pembroke and some others, a feature which is usually explained as a defence against mining though in this case probably built for extra strength. Inside, the hall was on the second storey, as would be expected, with the solar (private apartments) above and a small chapel on the top floor. The chapel is an irregular hexagon, being

extended into one of the buttresses. Otherwise, the buttresses are virtually solid. The tower is constructed of limestone ashlar and has remarkably few openings on the outside; even arrow loops are few and far between. Altogether, it is a formidable structure, though the fact that the castle was never besieged also contributes to its fine state of preservation. Much of the curtain wall, with half-section round towers, still stands, together with fragments of the barbican.

The castle was very advanced for its day. It was built between 1163, when Conisbrough came into the possession of Hamelin Plantagenet, an illegitimate half-brother of Henry II, and 1190. The mound on which it stands is basically natural, though banked up when the moat was made. There were earlier fortifications dating from pre-Conquest times.

Opposite: The White Tower at Conisburgh is visible for miles around and its roof offers a superb viewpoint of the surrounding area which has, sadly, changed since this romanticised, pre-industrial Revolution engraving was executed.

Below: An early nineteenth-century engraving of the ruined keep tower at Conisbrough Castle with fireplaces, hand-basins and garderobes visible in the walls.

CONWY

As at Caernarvon, town and castle at Conwy are closely integrated, the walls which surround the town having been built at the same time as the castle. Unusually, the walls, like the castle, are still in place. They stretch for nearly a mile with twenty-one round towers and three gates.

The Romans used to collect mussels from the Conwy estuary for their pearls, and there are still a few fishing boats operating. Conwy itself is a medieval town: a sixteenth-century print presents a view easily recognizable today, with the late-medieval house of Aberconwy at the junction of Castle and High streets. Another attraction is Plas Mawr ('Great House'), a relatively unaltered Elizabethan mansion. The town is also famous for its pioneering bridges: Telford's suspension bridge of 1826, its supports in the form of castellated towers in sympathy with the castle, and Stephenson's railway bridge of 1848.

At Deganwy, to the north, there was a fort which, legend says, was built by a Celtic king in the sixth century. A Norman castle also built here was smashed by Llywelyn ap Gruffydd in 1262 and few traces remain. The present castle, planned or overseen by the great Savoyard military engineer, James of St George, was virtually completed in a mere five years, 1283–7, displacing a Cistercian abbey. Like Caernarvon, Conwy is an 'enclosure' castle (no central tower or keep), and looks from a distance like a mighty cluster of giant towers. Over seventy feet high, with walls fifty feet thick, the towers are set at close intervals in the equally massive curtain wall. The overall plan is an irregular rectangle, adapted to fit the rock on which the castle is built, divided internally by a north–south wall between two of the towers into two wards or baileys. The main residential rooms were in the towers; the great hall, 130 feet long, in the outer (western) bailey. The main entrance, in the east, and the rear entrance at the opposite end were protected by barbicans.

The Welsh, no doubt wisely, never attacked the castle, though Edward I was trapped there for a time during the revolt of 1294 by an unexpected rise in the river. It fell into disuse and was sold to Lord Conwy for £100 in 1628. Meanwhile, the castle had suffered its only siege—taken by Cromwell's Parliamentary forces in the Civil War—without sustaining much damage.

Opposite: When he planned Conwy Castle, Master James of St George allowed for a sea door so that the castle could be provisioned in the event of the Welsh cutting off the land approaches.

CORFE

Although only noble fragments remain of the castle, they form part of one of the most spectacular views in England. From the coast road along the ridge west of Swanage, you see on the left the sea and, on the right, the even line of the Purbeck hills suddenly interrupted by a gap. In the centre of the gap rises a shapely hill, and on top of the hill stands the ruined castle.

The village, also called Corfe Castle, was a substantial place in earlier times but today is mainly a tourist attraction. The attractive old houses and cottages are built, roofs and all, of grey Purbeck stone, and Corfe was a centre of the quarrying trade which supplied the same stone to medieval shrines, tombs and churches in many parts. The whole area, including the castle, was recently bequeathed by the Bankes family to the National Trust. There is a large model of the castle as it was in its prime in the back garden of a café opposite the magnificently gargoyled church.

Perhaps the most famous event connected with Corfe Castle is the murder of the 18-year old King Edward, said to have been engineered by Queen Elfrida, his stepmother, in 978. In general, Corfe has a gruesome history, and at various times important persons were imprisoned there, including King Edward II before he was moved to Berkeley and murdered.

The foundation of the medieval stone castle followed soon after the Norman Conquest. It was a favourite residence of King John and expanded considerably during his reign. Further additions were made in the thirteenth century, including the outer gate through which one enters today, and at that time Corfe must have been one of the strongest castles in England. Roughly triangular in plan, it was—largely due to frequent additions—a complex building which to some extent outgrew its site, the outer baileys stretching

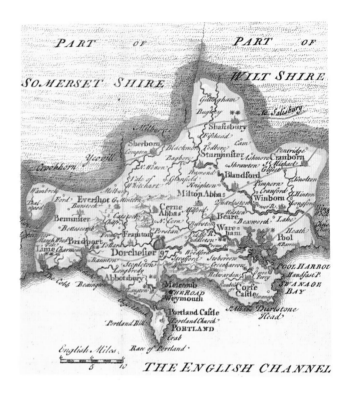

Above: Map of Dorset by Thomas Badeslade, 1742.

Opposite: The steep-sided hill on which Corfe was built was a splendid site for a fortress. This artist's impression shows the castle when it was flourishing, and in ruins after its destruction by Parliamentary forces.

down the hill. It is difficult to visualize it from the present ruins except with a plan.

Corfe ceased to be a royal castle in the sixteenth century when Elizabeth I, economizing as usual, sold it. In 1635 it passed to Sir John Bankes, the greatest landowner in the neighbourhood. During the Civil War it was held by Lady Bankes for the king during an epic siege. In 1646 it was destroyed by order of Parliament.

CRAIGMILLAR

Craigmillar Castle stands on the rising ground south of Edinburgh. When first built towards the end of the fourteenth century, it was situated in the country, and the immediate neighbourhood retains a wooded, rural aspect, though Craigmillar has now been overlapped by the Edinburgh suburbs. The castle was built by Sir Simon Preston of Gorton and remained in the possession of this prominent family, thereafter the Prestons of Craigmillar, until sold in 1660. The arms of the family carved in stone, which formerly stood over an arch, were described by Scott: 'three unicorns head-couped, with cheese press and barrel or tun—a wretched rebus to express their name of Preston' ('pressed tun'). Some of the buildings postdate the 1660 sale, but the oringinal L-plan tower house, though ruined, still stands. It is surrounded by walls, erected in the fifteenth century, with round corner towers and formidable machicolation. The outer walls, with a somewhat redundant moat, were built in the sixteenth century, after the castle had been burned by the English in 1544 during the episode named with characteristic Scottish irony the 'Rough Wooing'. A nineteenth century authority remarked that 'there is, perhaps, no other instance in Scotland of a family mansion so systematically built on the principles of fortification in the sixteenth century.'

Perceptive visitors can observe a well-worn stone step which bears a groove apparently made by some metal instrument. The guide, if he considers his listeners sufficiently gullible, may inform them that this was where the executioner's axe was sharpened. The cook's carving knife seems a more likely culprit, but the castle has its share of grim tales. It was here that the Earl of Mar, brother of James III, died in 1479, allegedly by opening his veins in the bath in preference to an even cruder demise offered by his brother. In the sixteenth century the castle was often visited by royalty, both James V and Mary apparently using it as a kind of retreat. Mary was at Craigmillar after the murder of Rizzio. Some say she met Bothwell there, and that she plotted to lure Darnley to Craigmillar to bring about his death. However, he died at Kirk o' Field.

Opposite: Craigmillar Castle was destroyed on Henry VIII's orders, but was restored by the time Mary, Queen of Scots arrived from France in 1561. By the eighteenth century, however, it had fallen into disrepair.

Below: The arms of the Preston family who owned Craigmillar Castle until 1660 can clearly be seen in the carving in the foreground of this engraving.

DONNINGTON

High on a spur of the Berkshire Downs north of Newbury stands all that remains of Donnington Castle. It is a lofty gatehouse, with twin towers nearly seventy feet high. The windows above the entrance are relatively large, and betray the fact that this was less a fortress than a residence.

The medieval manor house was fortified, with royal permission, by Richard de Abberbury, a court official, in 1386. Buildings were ranged around a roughly rectangular courtyard, with towers at the four corners and in the centre of the north and south walls, and the gatehouse, probably the last structure to be completed, in the east. It has been suggested that William de Wynford, who built the nave of Winchester Cathedral, may have been involved in the plan, which was somewhat similar to that of Bodiam (p 28)— under construction at the same time. Donnington's military pretensions were perhaps secondary; it was described 200 years after its founding as 'small but very neat' with 'windows on all sides being very lightsome'.

Donnington Castle's chief historic interest lies in the notable part it played in the Civil War when, as a result of its location overlooking the main road to Oxford, the king's headquarters, it was under siege off and on for the best part of two years. Obviously it was not the sort of building that could be expected to withstand serious attack by artillery, and the reason for its long resistance lay in the sophisticated defenceworks of earth and timber that were constructed by Sir John Boys, who held it for the king.

Parliamentary forces laid siege to the castle in July 1644. A direct attack failed, but three of the towers were flattened by artillery fire. The advance of the royalist forces from the west ended the siege and earned Boys his knighthood. There followed the second battle of Newbury, a drawn-out affair in which the castle protected the royalist flank. Charles escaped

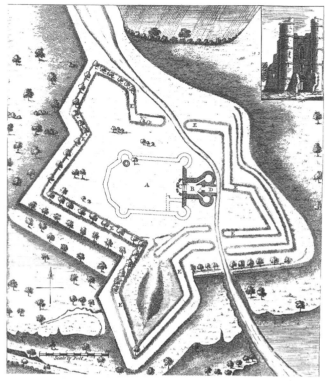

by night, leaving his artillery safe in the castle, and the siege was renewed. The attackers resorted to poisoning the wells, but at least warned the garrison, and in November the king brought relief again, before withdrawing his reclaimed artillery. More of the fortifications were destroyed, but the earthworks were reinforced and Boys held out until after the king's cause was lost, surrendering in April 1646.

Above: The earthworks – E in this ground plan of Donnington Castle – were built during the Civil War when Parliamentarians laid siege to the castle for two years.

Opposite: Even in ruins, Donnington Castle presents a forbidding facade to the world, and it is not difficult to see how it withstood four sieges during the Civil War before surrendering in 1645.

Below: The twin-towered gatehouse at Donnington is the sole remnant of the Berkshire castle that overlooked the old London–Bath road.

DOUNE

The little town of Doune, about nine miles north-west of Stirling, has made many contributions to Scottish history. Its craftsmen were once famous for pistols, and there were also connections with the clothing trade: King James IV's tailor was responsible for the sixteenth-century bridge over the River Teith. In more recent times, the agricultural pioneer James Smith conducted experiments here and invented, among other useful things, the salmon ladder, which enables fish to circumnavigate weirs on their way upstream to the spawning grounds.

Doune Castle was built by that formidable figure, Robert Stewart, Duke of Albany and the most powerful figure in Scotland, who was later regent for the young (and absent—the English had grabbed him) James I, in the late fourteenth century. The site had been fortified before, possibly since the Iron Age. The most impressive feature of the castle is the four-sided tower in the north-east corner, almost 100 feet high, with an attached turret commanding the entrance that is of approximately equal height. The remainder of the north side is fully taken up by powerful buildings once occupied by the garrison, and guarded by another turret. A second substantial tower stands in the centre of the west side. It contains the enormous kitchen, with eighteen-foot fireplace, suggesting large parties entertained by Albany. The courtyard, to the south of the main block, is surrounded by a thick curtain wall, about forty feet high.

The castle's present fine state of preservation is largely due to restoration in the late nineteenth and twentieth centuries. However, it was sympathetically done, and in 1500 the castle must have looked much like it does now. In fact, it was never seriously damaged except by neglect. When King James finally returned to Scotland in 1525 Albany was top of his hit list. The old duke was dead, but his son and successor was executed and the castle confiscated. It was returned to the family in the late sixteenth century, shortly before they acquired the title earl of Moray. The castle was used at various times as a residence for royal dowagers and as a prison—for instance by the Jacobites during the rebellion of 1745. Nevertheless, it fell eventually into ruins, from which it has now re-emerged.

Opposite: Jacobite soldiers used Doune Castle as a prison during the '45 rising after which it was allowed to crumble into the ruins seen in this engraving.

Below: Doune Castle takes its name from *dun*, meaning fortified town, and there are traces of prehistoric earthworks close to this imposing stone castle.

DOVER

The castle, one of England's greatest, stands high on the famous white cliffs above the port. Few military sites are older, for a Celtic hill fort was here before the Roman Conquest. A Roman *pharos*, or lighthouse, still stands within the walls, serving as bell tower for the Saxon church of St Mary in Castro (restored from near ruin in the nineteenth century).

In spite of an eventful history, the castle is well preserved, having played a continual military role into the present century. During the First World War it was the headquarters of the Dover Patrol, which endeavoured to keep U-boats out of the Straits. During the Second World War it was damaged not only by bombs but by German long-range artillery stationed in France.

After the Norman Conquest, William I's half-brother, Bishop Odo of Bayeux, erected a fort near Dover harbour from prefabricated parts brought from Normandy. The tremendous tower or keep was built by Henry II and the fortifications greatly enlarged and strengthened by his successors, especially Henry III, after the French had successfully mined one of the towers.

Some of the towers were shortened during the Napoleonic wars and made into gun platforms, rather spoiling the profile for what proved unnecessary reasons. The huge brick shelters constructed to house the troops who would repel Napoleon's invading army can still be seen on the western heights.

The scruffy seafront of pre-Victorian Dover is scarcely recognizable as the site of the castle-like ferries which today cross the Channel to France every few minutes. As the port closest to the Continental mainland, Dover has been of prime strategic and commercial significance since 1066, when it was already a town of some size. It continued to prosper, with occasional alarms during the frequent French

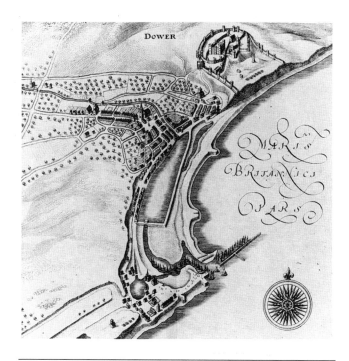

Above: This plan of Dover (Merien *c.*1650) shows the castle dominating Dover Harbour, with its walls extending right down to the edges of the famous white cliffs.

Opposite: Dover can rightly be called a 'growth' castle: the original twelfth-century keep-and-curtain design has embraced improvements spanning four centuries, the last being added by Henry VIII.

wars, throughout the Middle Ages. A statute of 1465 made Dover the only legal point of embarkation for Calais, and the London–Dover road was the busiest in the country. The people of Dover, as citizens of the Cinque Ports, provided twenty ships for the Royal Navy, but were relieved of certain other impositions. The main trades of the town were, not surprisingly, connected with maritime commerce. Dover was extensively reconstructed after the Second World War. Cross-channel traffic remains big business, and is unlikely to be destroyed by the Channel Tunnel which emerges a few miles along the coast at Folkestone, in Kent.

DUNSTANBURGH

It used to be said that the finest kippers come from the little Northumbrian fishing village of Craster, where there are now, in summertime at least, more holidaymakers than fishermen. A mile or so north of the village, standing on cliffs 100 feet above the sea, are the remains of one of the largest castles in the North of England, the great Lancastrian fortress of Dunstanburgh. Its long-ruined buildings cover an area of nearly ten acres.

Though an earlier stronghold probably stood on the site, the castle was built in the early fourteenth century by Thomas, Earl of Lancaster, a grandson of Henry III and the leader of the baronial opposition to Edward II and the Despensers. Thomas was later captured at the battle of Boroughbridge (1322) and executed at Pontefract. The site was guarded on two sides by the sea; and by making use of a handy gully and digging a ditch, eighty feet wide and thirteen feet deep, which terminated in Embleton Bay to the north, it was made virtually into an island. Further construction took place towards the end of the century under John of Gaunt, son of Edward III and Duke of Lancaster, who had married the heiress to the dukedom. During the Wars of the Roses, Dunstanburgh, like nearby Alnwick (p 14) and Bamburgh (p 20), was held for the Lancastrian cause, but it was forced to surrender in 1464. And that was more or less the end of its history—an active career of less than 150 years—for it was never restored and gradually fell into ruins. By the time it was painted by Turner in the early nineteenth century, it was in much the same state as it is today: rather worse, in fact, because some repairs have been done since in order to maintain the integrity of the surviving remains.

Despite 500 years of neglect, these remains are considerable, including a good deal of the walls with their projecting square towers, and in particular the massive gatehouse, with its twin round towers. The gatehouse became the main residential building in the time of John of Gaunt, who added a new gate with protecting barbican. Though reduced to half their original height, the dimensions of the towers give a convincing impression of impregnability.

Opposite: The dramatic silhouette of Dunstanburgh Castle outlined against the North Sea. Its wild and isolated location remains accessible only by a mile-long walk across moorland.

Below: The massive gatehouse of Dunstanburgh and some ruined walls are all that remain of the impregnable fortress that once sprawled over nine acres of the clifftops of Northumberland.

DUNVEGAN

Dunvegan has been the home of the chiefs of Clan MacLeod for about 700 years and is today the scene of an annual gathering when MacLeods from all over the world flock to Skye. It is as emotive a symbol of the history of the Highlands as can be found anywhere.

The MacLeods are said to be descended from Leod (which allegedly stems from an old Norse word meaning 'ugly'), son of Olaf the Black (died 1327), King of Man, who acquired Harris, Lewis and part of Skye by marriage. The two main branches of the clan, of Harris and of Lewis, derive from Leod's sons, Tormod and Torquil. Dunvegan is said to have been built by Leod himself. It stands at the head of a sea loch, facing Harris, and could only be entered by a sea gate guarded by a portcullis. The landward side was a sheer wall, even lacking windows until after the Jacobite Rebellion of 1745. Though extensively restored in the nineteenth century, Dunvegan is no beauty even now, but it is a treasure trove of clan history. Among the more arcane treasures is the so-called Fairy Flag, only to be unfurled in case of extreme danger, which is said to be of Byzantine origin. The famous chief, Alasdair *Crotach*, had to unfurl it twice during desperate battles with Clan Ranald in the early sixteenth century.

The MacLeods were not the only power on Skye. The ancient, now ruined castle of Duntulm was the seat of MacDonald chieftains, while MacDonald of Sleat held sway in the 'garden of Skye', but after the collapse of the Lordship of the Isles in the fifteenth century, Dunvegan became probably the chief centre of Gaelic culture—this is one of the few districts where Gaelic is still spoken as an everyday language. In the seventeenth century the MacLeods supported the Stewarts until the Battle of Worcester (1651), for which they provided 700 men of whom about three-quarters were killed. After that disaster, no MacLeod chief fought for the Stewarts again, and in 1745, when MacDonald of Sleat also held aloof (it was MacDonald of Kingsburgh who gave succour to Bonnie Prince Charlie on Skye), the chief raised a company in Hanoverian service, although there were a good number of MacLeods serving in Jacobite regiments. After that, the clan dwindled and scattered, but in 1935 Dame Flora MacLeod of MacLeod became chief and revived the spirit of the clan.

Opposite: The landward side of Dunvegan Castle, being more vulnerable to attack than the lochside, was built as a sheer wall with hardly any windows.

Above: A ground plan of Dunvegan Castle. The sea gate enabled supplies to be brought into the castle if the landward entries were blocked by enemies.

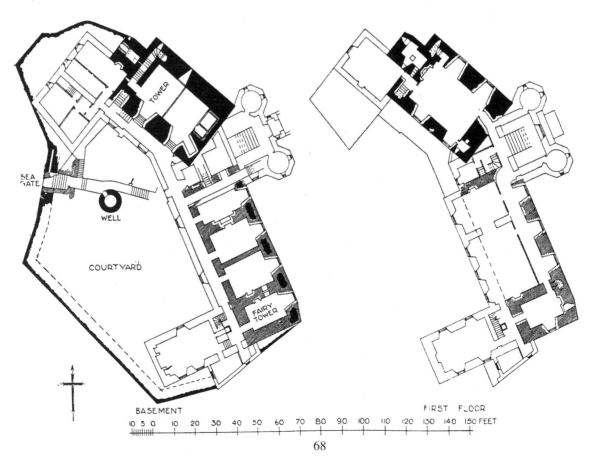

BASEMENT

FIRST FLOOR

10 5 0   10   20   30   40   50   60   70   80   90   100   110   120   130   140   150 FEET

DURHAM

At Durham the River Wear forms a loop around a steep, rocky peninsula. Crowning the summit is one of the most magnificent sights in England, the cathedral of Durham, possibly the finest piece of Romanesque (Norman) architecture in the country.

In the Middle Ages the bishop of Durham was an immensely potent figure, a prince-bishop of a type better known in Germany than England, who wielded virtually all the powers held elsewhere by the king. No doubt the king would have been less generous to the bishop of Durham, who acquired vast estates from the Crown, had it not been for the fact that while he was supposed to be elected by the monks, the king generally told the monks whom they should elect.

County Durham was a palatinate before the Norman Conquest, and part of the bishop's prestige stemmed from the connection with St Cuthbert (died 687) whose body was brought to Durham in the late tenth century. Politically, the importance of Durham lay in its strategic position on the road between England and the North. Invaders, from both directions, tended to pass this way, and Durham's history during the Middle Ages is largely one of turmoil, the bishop himself sometimes leading his army into battle. The bishop's palatine powers were severely curtailed by the Tudors, and though they were not finally abolished until the nineteenth century, the days of great feudal princes were by then long over. (Traces of the bishop's eminence remain: it is he who stands at the right hand of the monarch during the coronation.) The city itself, despite its famous festive associations with coal miners, never attracted industrial development, and it is still one of the most attractive of medieval English cities.

The castle, protecting the northern side of the peninsula not guarded by the river, is now part of the University of Durham (founded 1832), though it is open to the public. Originally, it was the bishop's palace and was founded shortly before building began of the present cathedral in 1092. Of the original Norman structure only the chapel remains; practically everything else has been rebuilt, since the proprietors were not short of cash for improvements. The last major rebuilding occurred in the seventeenth century, but shifting foundations necessitated extensive works in the 1930s.

Opposite: Durham Castle was a bishop's palace rather than a fortress and sits with other ecclesiastical and public buildings on a peninsula surrounded by the River Wear. Cole and Roper town plan, *c*.1801.

Below: Despite extensive rebuilding and refurbishment, Durham Castle still contains some of the finest examples of Romanesque architecture in Britain.

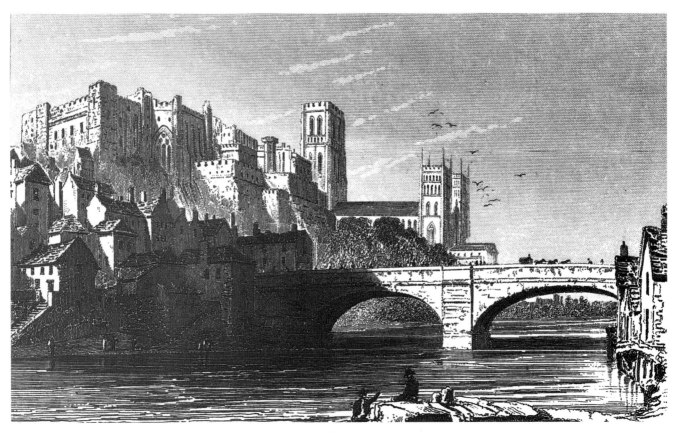

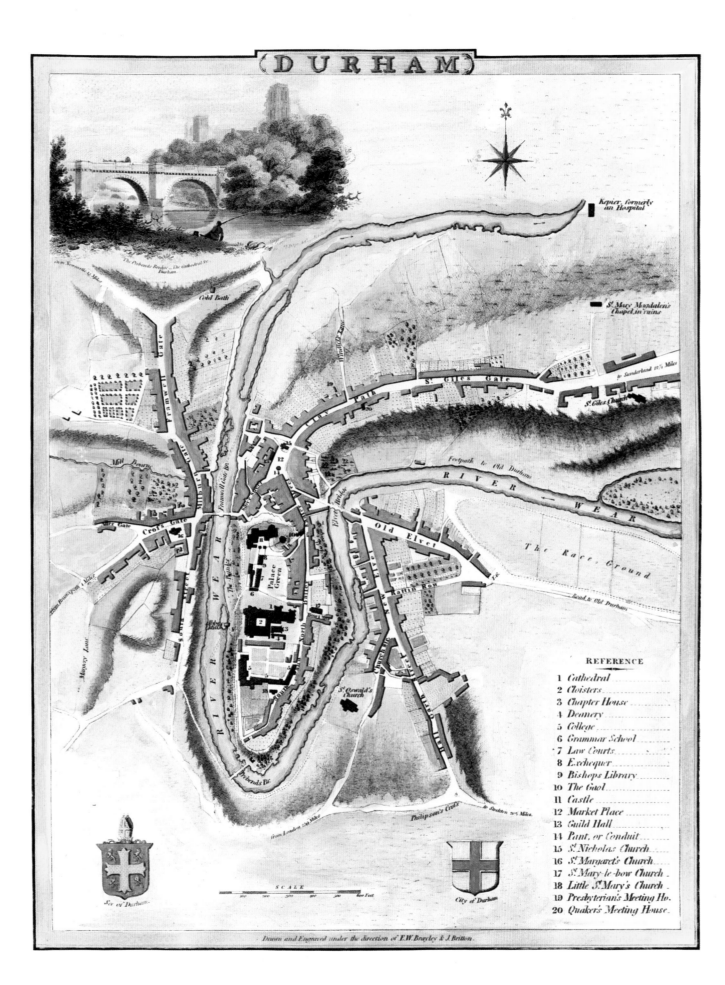

(DURHAM)

Kepier, formerly an Hospital

St. Mary Magdalen's Chapel in ruins

to Sunderland 12¼ Miles

St. Giles Church

St. Giles Gate

Footpath to Old Durham

RIVER WEAR

The Race Ground

Road to Old Durham

Cold Bath

Framwell Gate

Mill Bourn

Mere Gate

Crofs Gate

South Street

RIVER WEAR

Old Elvet

Hatam Row

St. Oswald's Church

Prebends Br.

Philipson's Crofs

to Stockton 20½ Miles

From London 258 Miles

The Prebends Bridge — The Cathedral &c. Durham.

REFERENCE

1 Cathedral
2 Cloisters
3 Chapter House
4 Deanery
5 College
6 Grammar School
7 Law Courts
8 Exchequer
9 Bishops Library
10 The Gaol
11 Castle
12 Market Place
13 Guild Hall
14 Pant, or Conduit
15 St. Nicholas Church
16 St. Margaret's Church
17 St. Mary-le-bow Church
18 Little St. Mary's Church
19 Presbyterian's Meeting Ho.
20 Quaker's Meeting House

SCALE

See of Durham.

City of Durham.

Drawn and Engraved under the direction of E.W. Brayley & J. Britton.

EDINBURGH

Rising on a rock of volcanic basalt 300 feet above the city streets, Edinburgh Castle seems to have grown there. Though its role has varied, it has been a working castle virtually throughout the past thirteen centuries. It has therefore escaped ruin through neglect, while being frequently altered, enlarged, or attacked, so that little of the original medieval castle remains.

The first recorded fortress was built in the seventh century by the Northumbrian king, Edwin (from whom the city is named 'Edwin's Burgh'). The oldest remaining building in the castle is the tiny twelfth-century St Margaret's Chapel (26 X 10 feet), which survived the destruction ordered by Robert Bruce after his forces captured the castle from the English in 1314.

King David I added a tower house in the south-east about 1367, the base of which was incorporated in the Half Moon Battery, originally built in 1574 but subsequently reconstructed. The palace buildings date back to James IV but the castle was seldom used as a royal residence after Mary Queen of Scots. James IV was also responsible for the Great Hall with its magnificent hammerbeam roof. The esplanade was levelled in the mid-eighteenth century to provide a parade ground, 'a bow shot wide'. It is now the scene of the floodlit Military Tatoo held every year in late summer.

Notwithstanding its present imposing elegance, the city of Edinburgh has had a turbulent history, disputed for centuries by the English and the Scots, later torn by religious and civil conflicts. The medieval city grew up along the Royal Mile, between the castle and Holyrood. The King's Wall, built about 1450, encompassed a very small area, ending in the west a bow shot from the castle and in the east at the bottom of the High Street. The wall built after the disaster of Flodden (1513) included a larger area, but no one dared to live outside it. Hence the uniquely tall tenements of the Old Town (if you can't build out, build up), charming now but in the seventeenth century pestilential.

The Act of Union (1707) downgraded Edinburgh, but led to greater commercial prosperity, and the city at last expanded. In the late eighteenth century it was the 'Athens of the North', a leading centre of European culture, and the New Town blossomed as one of the most handsome pieces of urban development since the Romans.

Opposite: An eighteenth-century view of Edinburgh Castle as seen from one of the bustling streets on the south of the Castle Rock.

Below: Town plan of Edinburgh by Braun and Hogenberg, *c.* 1574. This engraving gives a false impression of the street widths which were in fact very narrow.

GLAMIS

Glamis is a small and pretty village about five miles from Forfar in the fertile valley of Strathmore, in what used to be the county of Angus. It contains a curious old carved stone said to be a monument to King Malcolm II and some attractive eighteenth-century cottages which have been converted into a fascinating museum of agricultural implements and the cottage technology of old times. Its most notable feature, however, is the magnificent pile of Glamis Castle, childhood home of the Queen Mother and birthplace of Princess Margaret.

The castle is a splendid example of the style named half humorously 'Scottish baronial', a kind of amalgam of the traditions of the Scottish tower house and the French Renaissance *château*, and comes as close as possibly any building in the British Isles to the largely illusionary idea of a Gothic castle represented in French miniatures of the fifteenth century—a filigree of aspiring spires and turrets.

Mockery would be misplaced. This is a splendid building, perhaps the finest private residence in Scotland, and although its seventeenth-century turrets and battlements are of dubious defensive capacity, the core of Glamis is a sturdy, no-nonsense fourteenth-century tower, and some parts are even

earlier. The Lyons (later Bowes-Lyons and earls of Strathmore) came into possession of Glamis (the 'i' is silent, the name being derived from the Gaelic *glamhus*, a strath or vale) in 1424, and it has remained with them virtually ever since. Its history goes back even further, perhaps to Macbeth, who was allegedly Thane of Glamis among other titles, and it was an occasional residence of several early kings of Scots, as well as James Edward, the 'Old Pretender', in 1715 and Sir Walter Scott in about 1791. Legends associated with the castle possibly owe something to the latter visitor. Besides ghosts, they include an alleged secret chamber, known only to the thane and his heir. A fourteenth-century iron yett still defends the main entrance. These massive grilles replaced the portcullis and were popular in Scotland and northern England.

Opposite: The home of the earls of Strathmore and Kinghorne, Glamis Castle was an appropriately regal birthplace of Princess Margaret Rose, the younger daughter of George VI and Queen Elizabeth whose father was the fourteenth earl.

Below: Remains of the original Glamis Castle have been incorporated into the baronial mansion, described as one of the most magnificent in Britain.

HARLECH

The castle dominates Tremadoc Bay, a formidable structure in light grey standstone built on a rocky hill which descends precipitously in the west. When built, it was designed to be supplied by sea, if necessary, and the remains of a sea gate can still be seen. However the sea has since receded, and golfers, caravanners, even the main road, intervene. The town is now a centre of tourism, with good bathing and beach and a large nature reserve. In the distance rise the spectacular mountains of Snowdonia. Harlech received its borough charter when the castle was built, and the population was possibly larger then than it is now, but settlement is ancient; a fort occupied the site of the castle long before and there are legends here of ancient British heroes of the *Mabinogion*.

Harlech is one of the four greatest of Edward I's Welsh castles, supervised by James of St George, who became its first constable. Like Conwy (p 54), it was built extremely fast, between 1283 and 1290. Like Beaumaris (p 22), it is a concentric castle, with an inner and outer bailey, requiring attackers to make two assaults. The nature of the site made it hard to approach from the north or from the west, where the rockface descended to the sea, and on the other sides it was protected by a moat excavated from solid rock. The inner bailey, roughly square, is surrounded by a curtain wall with immense round towers at each corner. Otherwise, the main structure is the great eastern gatehouse, the outward towers of which have walls twelve feet thick. Although Harlech was captured relatively often, it was only once taken by direct assault, even in the days of cannon.

Harlech fell to Owain Glyndwr during the last great Welsh revolt against the English in 1401, the garrison having been overcome by starvation and disease. Glyndwr made it his headquarters and held it until an English force drove him out in 1409 and captured his family, though not himself. In the Wars of the Roses, Queen Margaret took refuge at Harlech and the castle withstood a siege that lasted six years: its gutsy Lancastrian defenders are celebrated in the martial song, 'Men of Harlech' (written much later). Finally during the Civil War, Harlech was held for the king until long after he had surrendered himself to Cromwell's army. Unlike many royalist castles, it was not deliberately destroyed, but rapidly fell into ruin anyway. Today, its formidable exterior appearance has been restored.

Opposite: It took seven years and £2 million by today's values to build Harlech Castle. The end result dominated the area for miles around.

Below: John Speed's map of Harlech (1610–11) shows the concentric design of the castle, designed by the great castle builder Master James of St. George.

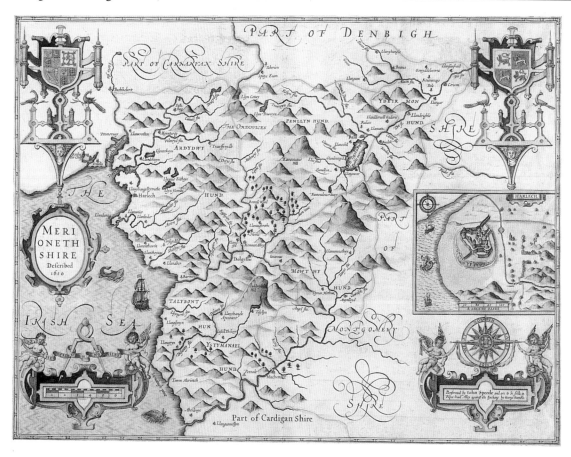

HERSTMONCEUX

Away from the coast, much of Sussex is very quiet and rural. Inland from Eastbourne and Hastings, there are no large towns and the villages are mostly very small. Two hundred years ago, things were more lively. The iron industry flourished; one of the last forges can still be seen at Ashburnham, near Herstmonceux, and there remain a few blacksmiths in the area, making wrought-iron gates and suchlike. The little villages, tucked away in comparative solitude but with easy access to the coast, were infested with smugglers. Most famous was the savage Hawkhurst Gang, powerful enough to wage war against the neighbouring village of Goudhurst without interference from the authorities. The Hawkhurst gang lost. The people of Goudhurst were forewarned of the planned assault and repelled the attackers from the church tower.

Hawkhurst is only a couple of miles north of Bodiam castle, and Herstmonceux (sometimes spelled Hurstmonceux) lies about fifteen miles farther to the south-west. The two castles have a certain family resemblance, although Herstmonceux is built of Flemish brick, rather than stone. Both are very regular in plan, centred on a massive gatehouse, and like Bodiam (p 8) Herstmonceux is surrounded by a moat so wide it is really a lake. However, Herstmonceux was built over half a century later, and that made a difference.

Sir Roger Fiennes received licence to build a fortified residence in 1441, when the age of the castle was fading, and Herstmonceux was more residence than fortress. It has all the features of a military stronghold, including machicolation, drawbridge, 'murder holes' in the ceiling above the entrance, and so on. However, the walls are relatively thin and, although there are arrow loops in the towers, there are also quite large windows. As the castle was never besieged, its defensive capacity was never put to the test.

The castle was abandoned in the late eighteenth century, its furnishings removed and some of the stone facings taken away to be used in other buildings. In this century it was carefully restored according to the original plans. The clear air—no industrial smog hereabouts—persuaded the Royal Observatory to move to Herstmonceux from Greenwich in 1948, but it has now moved out again.

Opposite: Despite its fortress-like appearance, Herstmonceux never saw any military action and was allowed to decay quietly from the eighteenth century until the twentieth century when it was splendidly rebuilt and restored.

Below: This engraving, dating from 1770, shows Herstmonceux before it fell into disrepair and masonry was removed to build nearby Herstmonceux House.

Kenilworth

The town of Kenilworth in Warwickshire, though mentioned in Domesday Book and known for its leather and dyes, is significant mainly as an adjunct to the famous castle, standing to the west of the town. This, though, unusually, not built on an impressive site, was once the greatest royal fortress in the English Midlands and covered an area of seven acres. Its ruined state notwithstanding, it is still one of the most impressive of all great English castles. In its remains one can read four centuries of history.

The estate was bestowed by Henry I on his chamberlain, Geoffrey de Clinton, who built a timber motte castle. His successor replaced this about 1170 or soon after with a great Norman tower much of which, altered in later times, still stands. Impressed by its strength, Henry II took it back into royal possession, and during the next three reigns it was much enlarged and improved. King John built a curtain wall, and Henry III created a system of water defences even larger than Caerphilly's (p 36). Traces remain in the form of marshy fields. Having made it all but impregnable, Henry bestowed it on his brother-in-law, Simon de Montfort, unwisely as things turned out, for within a few years he was forced to lay siege to it (in 1266, after Simon's death, the castle being held by his son). The water defences prevented mining, and long-distance siege machines failed to effect a breach. The battle waged furiously. Stone missiles hurled by giant catapults on either side collided in mid-air and shattered with explosive force, spraying chips like grapeshot. The defenders held out for six months but were overcome at last, not by the hurtling missiles, nor by the mobile towers containing 200 archers which the King sent against them, but by foes more insidious and, in siege warfare, more effective—General Starvation and Major Disease.

That epic siege apart, the castle is best remembered for altogether jollier events. In 1279 Roger de Mortimer arranged a famous tournament, which was attended by 100 knights and 100 ladies. In the late fourteenth century the castle came into the hands of John of Gaunt, who turned it into a sumptuous palace-castle, as is evident from the remains of his great hall. How closely the works were directed by the great Lancastrian prince is a moot point; for a man who spent a large part of his life abroad John of Gaunt is credited with a remarkable amount of castle building in England.

Opposite: An attractive county map by Thomas Moule including decorative sketches of Kenilworth and Warwick castles.

Below: The romantic ruins of Kenilworth Castle. Despite its state of disrepair it remains one of the most impressive and romantic of all of English castles.

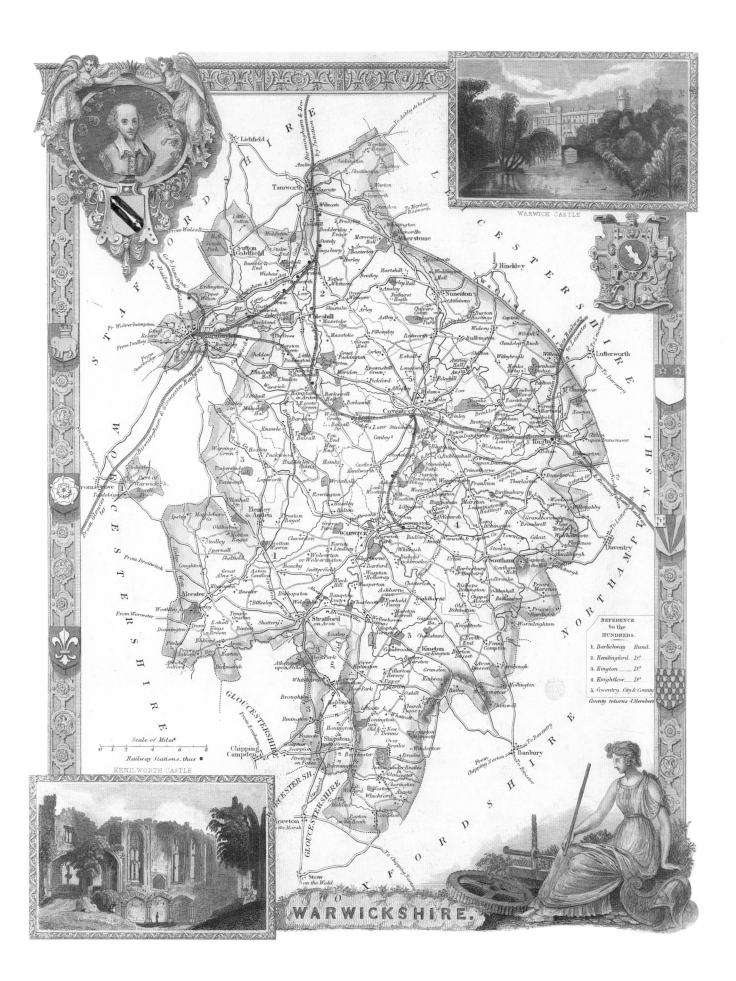

WARWICK CASTLE

KENILWORTH CASTLE

Scale of Miles*
0 1 2   4   6   8
• Railway Stations, thus •

REFERENCE
to the
HUNDREDS.
1. Barlichway   Hund.
2. Hemlingford   D.º
3. Kington   D.º
4. Knightlow   D.º
5. Coventry City & County

County returns 4 Members

WARWICKSHIRE.

The castle's most flamboyant days were still to come. In 1563 Queen Elizabeth bestowed it on her favourite, Robert Dudley, Earl of Leicester, and that extravagant courtier made further extensive additions and alterations. He erected the great gatehouse in the north, which is the only part of the castle still lived in today, heightened and enhanced the old Norman tower, and built the range of buildings known as 'Leicester's Buildings'. He also laid out the formal gardens, complete with nude nymphs that raised the hackles of proto-Puritans. In 1575 he threw one of the world's most expensive parties at Kenilworth for the benefit of the queen: it lasted nineteen days at a reported cost of £1,000 a day – a sum, no doubt greatly exaggerated, that would have exceeded the total royal revenue. The entire visit was like an ongoing masque, with Classical or Arthurian figures popping up unexpectedly to proclaim verses in praise of the distinguished visitor. There was feasting (300 dishes at one banquet), fireworks, music and dancing. A mermaid emerged from the lake one day to surprise the queen as she returned from hunting. The Lady of the Lake was impersonated by a boy actor (there was an eleven-year-old future actor in the county called William Shakespeare but alas it was not he), who was conveyed about his, or her, domain on a floating island lit with torches. Classical marine deities appeared on a model dolphin which had an orchestra concealed within it.

After the Civil War the castle was ordered to be dismantled, and though the job was not done as thoroughly as in some other places, it was never inhabited again. It passed to various private owners before Sir John Siddely bought it in 1937 and gave it to the nation. As Scott moralized, 'the massive ruins … impress upon the visitor the transitory value of human possessions and the happiness of those who enjoy a humble lot in virtuous contentment', from which we may suppose that the laird of Abbotsford would have been perfectly happy in a medieval peasant's hut ….

Opposite: Although it is now in ruins, the remains of Kenilworth Castle, especially the Great Hall with its glorious oriel windows, give some idea of its past magnificence.

Below: More than 100 years before this ground plan of Kenilworth was printed, the castle had been destroyed by the victorious Parliamentarians.

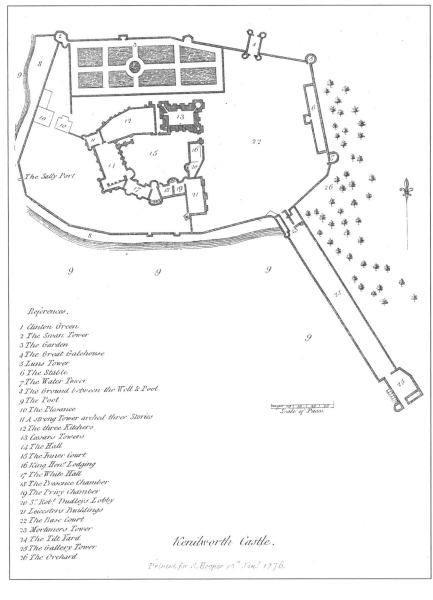

References.

1 Clinton Green
2 The Swan Tower
3 The Garden
4 The Great Gatehouse
5 Luns Tower
6 The Stable
7 The Water Tower
8 The Ground between the Well & Pool
9 The Pool
10 The Plesance
11 A strong Tower arched three Stories
12 The three Kitchens
13 Cæsars Tower
14 The Hall
15 The Inner Court
16 King Hen.ª Lodging
17 The White Hall
18 The Presence Chamber
19 The Privy Chamber
20 S.ʳ Rob.ᵗ Dudleys Lobby
21 Leicesters Buildings
22 The Base Court
23 Mortimers Tower
24 The Tilt Yard
25 The Gallery Tower
26 The Orchard

Kenilworth Castle.

Printed for S. Hooper 20.ᵗʰ Jan.ʸ 1776.

LANCASTER

Glancing westward from the M6, the passing motorist can easily locate Lancaster from the distinctive dome of the Aston Memorial (1909), commemorating the family who bequeathed the pleasant park in which it stands.

The capital of the old county palatine of Lancaster lies on the River Lune, just above its estuary. There was a time when it was a port handling more cargo than Liverpool, and the old Custom House is one of many surviving eighteenth-century buildings. Earlier times are also commemorated, notably by the castle and the priory church, containing famous carved stalls in the choir, which stand together on Castle Hill. However, few traces remain of the Roman camp which gave the town its name (from the Latin *castrum*), or of its Saxon successor.

Both the castle and the priory were founded by Roger de Poictou about the end of the eleventh century; part of the Norman keep survives. Edmund 'Crouchback', 1st Earl of Lancaster, received Lancaster from his father, Henry III, in 1267, and the present gatehouse—the most substantial medieval remnant, with twin octagonal towers, machicolations and portcullis—was largely the result of rebuilding during the late fourteenth century in the time of John of Gaunt, though it was altered again in the sixteenth century. John, named after Ghent, his birthplace, was the chief progenitor (after Edmund)

of the Lancastrian dynastic line. A lookout tower at the corner of the keep is known as 'John of Gaunt's Chair', and the arms of his son Bolingbroke (King Henry IV) can be seen on the gatehouse.

Lancaster Castle is one of those which has remained in almost continual use, resulting in frequent alteration and reconstruction, so that the predominant impression today is less medieval than nineteenth-century. The Shire Hall is very baronial in appearance, but it was built in 1802. As a fortress, the castle survived attack by Robert Bruce, who smashed the town, and it was held for Parliament during the Civil War, withstanding more than one royalist attack. Thereafter, it was used as a prison and courthouse. The Dungeon Tower, on the south side, was pulled down in 1812 but subterranean cells may still be seen: ten women condemned as witches were held here and subsequently executed on Gallows Hill in the reign of the superstitious James I.

Opposite: Promenading in the grounds of Lancaster Castle was a popular pastime among the *beau monde* of the city in the nineteenth century.

Below: This Speed map features portraits of the rival houses of the Lancastrians and Tudors, as well as a plan of the city of Lancaster.

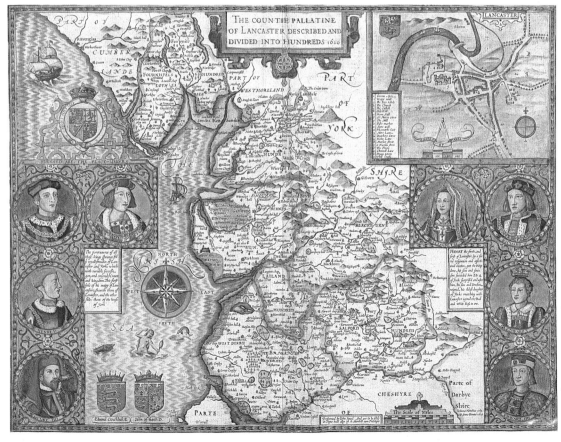

LAUNCESTON

In the Middle Ages Launceston, just across the Devon border, was the most important town in Cornwall. Helped by its hilly situation, it remains an attractive, unspoiled, and relatively traffic-free town today, with many medieval remains. Perhaps its most interesting building is the church of St Mary Magadalene, built at the beginning of the sixteenth century—apart from the detached fourteenth-century tower—whose granite exterior is almost entirely covered with low-relief sculpture. Some parts of the medieval town wall also exist, including the arches of the south gate. The castle, poised on a very large mound, was the seat of the royal earls (later dukes) of Cornwall. It suffered much damage during the later stages of the Civil War as the royalists, strong in Cornwall, made valiant efforts to hold it but, though ruined, the remains today are well preserved and maintained by English Heritage.

Launceston had a mint and a market before the Norman Conquest. The Conqueror's brother, Robert of Mortmain, built a timber motte castle on the summit soon after the Conquest, perhaps replacing an earlier fort. About one hundred years later a roughly circular shell keep was constructed and, another fifty years after that, a new tower, built of quite different stone from the shell keep, was erected inside it. The area between the tower and shell keep was

roofed over, and though the roof has long gone, the walls are still standing, as well as a stairway up the tower from the top of which there is a fine view over the town. A low, outer wall was also built; this has now vanished, and what was the bailey is an agreeable park. The castle was said to be in poor condition when Edward the Black Prince inherited it. He carried out some renovation and added the north gatehouse. Excavation has revealed a large stone hall in the bailey which may date from this period and was built on the foundations of earlier, eleventh-century structures.

In spite of the near destruction of the castle in the Civil War, it was not totally abandoned. It was used as a prison for a time, one of its occupants being the Quaker leader, George Fox, arrested for distributing pamphlets for the Society of Friends in 1656.

Opposite: Although ruined, overgrown with ivy and affording pasture for cattle, something of the grandeur of Launceston Castle survives in this eighteenth-century engraving.

Below: John Speed's superb map of Cornwall includes a view of the ancient town of Launceston and, to the right, a panel showing natural features and archaeological remains. Note the royal arms above the title.

LEEDS

Leeds Castle in Kent is one of the most picturesque buildings in south-east England, built on two adjacent islands in the River Len, a lake being formed by a fourteenth-century dam. There was a wooden fort here, attacked by the Vikings in the ninth century, and the first stone castle was built early in the twelfth century. It was violently disputed during the wars between Stephen and Matilda, and scarcely a trace remains. Leeds has been constantly inhabited since then, which means that, inevitably, it has been much rebuilt. Most of what the visitor to the castle sees today is the result of nineteenth-century restoration.

A major building programme took place under Edward I: an outer curtain wall reinforced by half-round towers, a water gate, a new gatehouse in the south-west, and rebuilding of the Gloriette, a large, low D shaped tower on the smaller island. The walls of the Gloriette, raised a storey by Henry VIII, still stand. Edward gave the castle to Queen Eleanor and later to his second wife, starting the tradition that gave Leeds the nickname 'Dames Castle'. It was besieged during the reign of Edward II, having been bestowed on a vassal who turned rebellious, then held for a time by Edward's unloving queen, Isabella. One of the men involved in subsequent improvements was the famous royal mason, Henry Yevele (died 1400), designer of Westminster Hall and (probably) the nave at Canterbury. The last queen to hold Leeds was Katherine de Valois, wife of Henry V, who after her royal husband's death secretly contracted a marriage with a humble official, Owen Tudor. Their grandson was to gain the throne as Henry VII after the Battle of Bosworth.

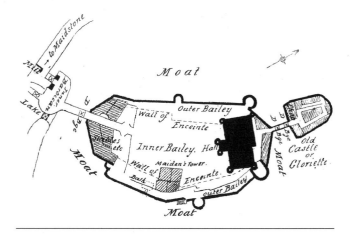

Above: Leeds Castle stands on two islands as can be seen from this ground plan. The smaller island contains the D-shaped tower complex (*gloriette*) and is connected to the main castle by a drawbridge.

Opposite: Leeds may have the appearance of a centuries-old fortress, but much of its 'medieval' defences were put up in the nineteenth century shortly before this engraving was done.

The progress from fortress to palace was completed by Henry VIII, who had large casement windows installed and built the 'Maidens Tower', but subsequently bestowed Leeds on Sir Anthony St Leger. The nineteenth-century work was done by Fiennes Wykeham-Martin, who demolished the outer walls to improve the view. In 1926 it was bought by Olive, Lady Baillie. She devoted years to the restoration and improvement of the castle and bequeathed it to the nation at her death, in 1974, on condition that it should also serve as a conference centre, for medical research in particular. It contains many wonderful rooms and objects, from medieval dog collars to modern paintings.

LUDLOW

Shropshire is one of the most beautiful counties in England, and Ludlow, situated among hills and woods where the River Corve joins the Teme, one of its most attractive towns. Although there are stories of earlier settlement, the town seems to have developed with the Norman castle. It was a prosperous place about the fifteenth century, thanks to the patronage of the House of York, and retains much of its original street plan, with many fine houses dating from the fifteenth to the eighteenth centuries. They include a congenial half-timbered inn and a massive church, its tower outreaching the castle, with a fifteenth-century east window and the grave of A. E. Housman in the churchyard.

The castle, on a rocky hill above the River Teme, was originally a border fortress and later headquarters of the Council of the Marches. It was dismantled in the wake of the English Civil War, but the ruins are well preserved, and this is among the most rewarding castles in England for visitors, offering an easily assimilable lesson in English military architecture. It was one of the earliest examples of a castle built with a curtain wall flanked by towers at the corners.

Founded by Roger de Lacey within twenty years of the Norman Conquest, it was enlarged or altered at various times up to the Elizabethan age, when Sir Henry Sidney (father of Philip) presided over the Council of the Marches in some state. He also indulged in extensive rebuilding, completing the castle's gradual progress from fortress to administrative centre and palace (Milton's *Comus* was first performed here in 1634). Sir Henry's coat of arms may still be seen above the gateway to the great hall. Of the remaining buildings, the most unusual is the chapel, which has one of the few circular naves in England, built by Sir Joyce de Dynan in the mid-twelfth century.

In the colourful and turbulent history of Ludlow Castle, two sad dynastic events stand out. Here Arthur Prince of Wales, son of Henry VII, brought his bride, Catherine of Aragon, only to die soon afterwards, bequeathing his bride to his younger brother Henry. Earlier, Ludlow was the last residence of the young Edward V and his still younger brother, the Duke of York, before they were moved in 1483 to another Norman stronghold, the Tower of London (p 114), never to be seen again.

Above: Ludlow Castle, seen here in an early nineteenth-century engraving, contains a Norman chapel modelled on the Church of the Holy Sepulchre in Jerusalem.

Opposite: Given its situation on the Welsh March, it is hardly surprising that the castle at Ludlow, featured in the decorative border of Thomas Moule's map of Shropshire, has had an exciting history.

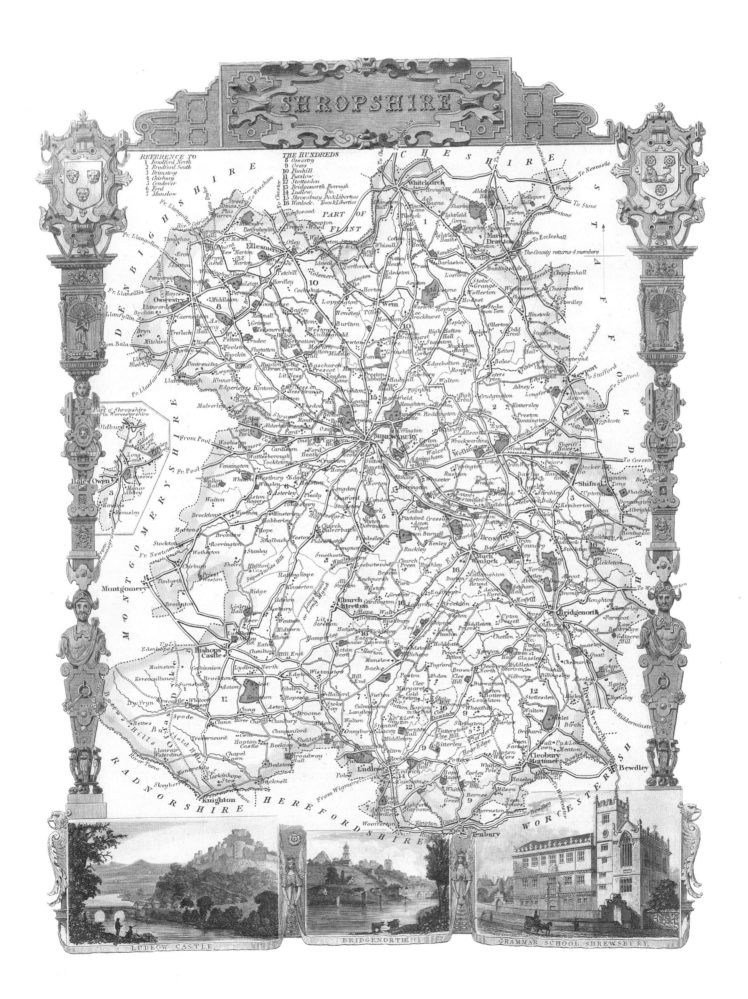

SHROPSHIRE

REFERENCE TO THE HUNDREDS
1 Bradford North
2 Bradford South
3 Brimstry
4 Chirbury
5 Condover
6 Ford
7 Munslow
8 Oswestry
9 Overs
10 Pimhill
11 Purslow
12 Stottesden
13 Bridgenorth Borough
14 Ludlow
15 Shrewsbury Do. & Liberties
16 Wenlock. Town & Liberties

LUDLOW CASTLE.

BRIDGENORTH.

GRAMMAR SCHOOL SHREWSBURY.

NORWICH

In Norwich, as at Rochester (p 104) and some other cities, Norman castle and Norman cathedral are close neighbours, nodding to each other across the roofs of humbler dwellings. The Art Deco city hall raises its red-brick clock tower in only feeble challenge, and the bulky Roman Catholic cathedral is too far away to make an impression. Though undergoing something of a revival, not totally welcome, in recent years, Norwich has been generally a quiet place since the Industrial Revolution. But in the Middle Ages, things were very different. Not only was it, from the days of the Vikings to Kett's Rebellion (1549), one of the most turbulent, it was also one of the largest provincial cities in England, probably *the* largest by the fifteenth century (though this is disputed in Bristol), being the administrative and market centre for a large part of East Anglia, the richest region in the kingdom thanks to wool.

The ascendancy of Norwich can be dated to 1094, the year that Bishop Herbert de Losinga decided to abandon Thetford and make Norwich the seat of his diocese. The stone castle replaced an earlier wooden one situated on a huge mound dominating the city which was begun slightly later. The stone for both castle and cathedral was imported from Caen in Normandy, coming up the River Wensum to within a few yards of the building site.

All that remains of the castle today is the impressive Norman tower or keep which, though often restored (notably by Anthony Salvin about 1830), probably looks from the outside much as it did when built, about 1120. It is almost square in plan, ninety or ninety-five feet along each wall, and nearly eighty feet high. A remarkable feature is the decoration of the walls with courses of blind arcading—perhaps influenced by the cathedral going up at the same time (but evident also at Castle Rising (p 44) on the other side of Norfolk). The castle has had many uses and only the shell of the Norman building remains. For the past hundred years it has been a museum which contains, among other exhibits, a large collection of the Dutch-influenced Norwich School of painters, virtually the only regional school in English art history, whose leading lights were John Crome (1768–1821) and J. S. Cotman (1782–1842).

Opposite: The imposing tower of Norwich Castle was built of blocks of stone quarried at Caen in Normandy, shipped across the Channel and up the east coast of England to the town - then one of the largest in England.

Below: A fine county map of Norfolk by John Speed with an inset town plan of Norwich, the largest provincial city in England in the fifteenth century.

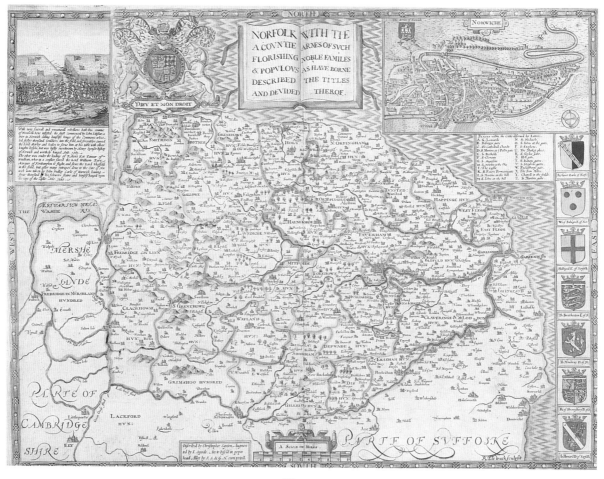

PEMBROKE

In the central Middle Ages, Pembroke was a strategically important place, the chief seat of the earls palatine of Pembroke and the most convenient port for Ireland. Town and castle grew up together, and the town was fortified along with the castle: many parts of the old walls remain and the medieval plan of the town is still visible—basically a single broad street, with the massive tower of St Mary's church in the centre. In the sixteenth century, after the formal union of England and Wales and the end of the palatinate, Pembroke's significance as a seat of government diminished, and it was soon superseded by Haverfordwest. Something of a revival came in the nineteenth century with the establishment of the naval dockyards at Milford Haven and the building of Pembroke Dock as a garrison town. Since the advent of the oil tanker, Milford Haven has regained its dominance.

The castle is one of the greatest pre-Edwardian castles in Britain. It was founded before 1200, replacing an earlier earthwork enclosure on a rocky peninsula in the estuary, by William Marshal, Earl of Pembroke. The most impressive feature of the castle today is the tower or keep, four storeys high, that he erected within a roughly triangular bailey. The tower has a markedly splayed base, a fairly common feature probably designed to buttress the walls, or to frustrate sappers, or to provide an angle to bounce missiles off from

the battlements—or perhaps all three. The bailey was protected on two of the three sides by water, on the third by a massive curtain wall. The gatehouse contained an astonishing series of portcullises and other defensive devices.

The castle, birthplace of Henry VII, saw exciting times during the Civil War, when Pembroke assumed special importance through King Charles's hope of getting help from Ireland. It was held for Parliament by the mayor of Pembroke, John Poyer, who withstood a siege unmoved by the Royalist general's threat to pack him in a barrel and roll him into the sea. However, when the army fell out with the Presbyterians, the governor, a Presbyterian, changed sides and as a result found himself again besieged, in 1648, by no less a figure than Cromwell himself. He held out for some time, but was forced to surrender when the water supply was cut off. Cromwell then reduced the castle to impotence.

Opposite: The great central tower of Pembroke Castle is 53 feet in diameter, rises to almost 80 feet tall and has walls over 16 feet thick in parts!

Below: The ground map of Pembroke Castle shows the position of the great keep that dominated the castle before it fell into disrepair, and still dominates the ruins that remain today.

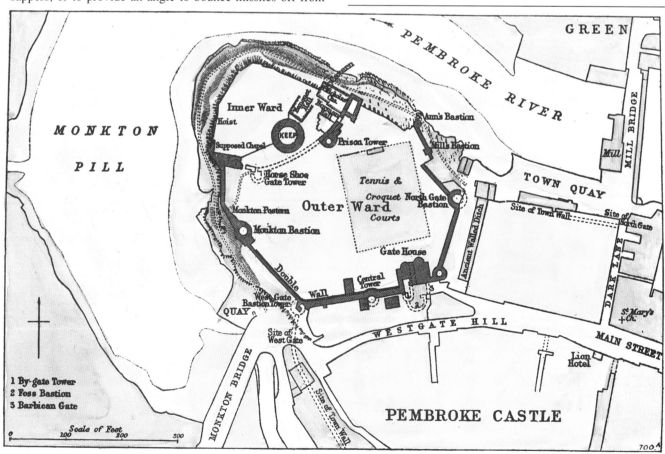

PORTCHESTER

Portchester (sometimes called Porchester) is on the north shore of Portsmouth harbour, backed by downs that command a view of the whole harbour. Its history has been largely determined by geology or climate, for when the Romans arrived in Britain in AD 43 sea levels were relatively high, and Portchester, where there was a sizable British settlement, appeared strategically more significant than it did later. However, when the sea receded, Portsmouth—which scarcely existed before the twelfth century—became the site of the great naval base that otherwise might have centred on Portchester.

On the level ground north of the bay, the Romans built a substantial fort for defence against seaborne invaders in the late third century. In plan it was a characteristically regular square, about 210 yards along each side, with D-plan bastions at frequent intervals. Astonishingly, these walls still stand to their full height today. The Norman castle, equally well-preserved (but nearly a thousand years younger), was built in the north-west corner. Rectangular, with buildings ranged on all four sides of the quadrangle, its main feature is the square tower—originally two storeys, later doubled in height—in the extreme corner. The inner Norman walls were protected by a moat and a gatehouse on the south side. Gatehouses were also built in the centre of the east and west Roman walls. An Augustinian priory was established in the south-east, opposite the castle, though it was soon abandoned, the present church of St Mary being the only survival. Portchester remained a royal castle into the seventeenth century. It was used as an assembly point for

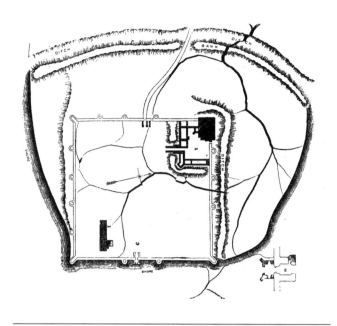

Above: The great tower of Portchester Castle is situated at the top right of this ground plan that shows very clearly the perfectly square wall of the Roman fortress built almost two thousand years ago when the Romans occupied Britain.

Opposite: In its heyday, Portchester Castle accommodated a small town, but when it grew too large for the confining Roman walls, it spread to the more spacious site of present-day Portsmouth.

troops during the Hundred Years War (1337–1453), and in the eighteenth century it housed captured French sailors. The castle was improved by various monarchs, notably Richard II, with his accustomed eye for beauty and comfort. The hall and kitchen date from his reign, though he does not seem to have spent much, if any, time at Portchester.

RAGLAN

North of the small village of Raglan, and about five miles west of Monmouth, stand the ruins of this magnificent castle that, at first glance, might have been built in the days of Edward I but actually dates from the mid-fifteenth century. This is border country, and castles are fairly thick on the ground: the 'Guardians of Gwent', Grosmont, Skenfrith and White Castle, are not far to the north, Monmouth and Chepstow (p 48) Castles to the east and south. Raglan undoubtedly stands on the site of a Norman fortress. No certain remains of it can be seen, although it may possibly be represented in the base of the main tower, which certainly stands on the site of a still earlier motte castle.

This tower, known as the 'Yellow Tower of Gwent', is the most interesting part. It was begun by Sir William ap Thomas, who had apparently made his money in the French wars, between about 1430 and 1445 (when Sir William died). Four storeys high, plus basement, it is hexagonal in plan, with an outer wall having half-round towers at the angles. The upper parts of the main tower are missing, but it presumably had the parapet and machiolation to be seen in the polygonal towers of the great gatehouse and curtain wall. It stands in a bailey surrounded by a moat and separate from the remainder of the castle, which mostly dates from the late fifteenth and sixteenth centuries and occupies an irregular rectangle to the north. The best-preserved building is the great hall, which with the chapel divided the quadrangle into two courts. It was probably part of the original construction, though its casement windows must have been inserted a century later.

Sir William's heir, who became Earl of Pembroke, supported the Yorkist cause in the Wars of the Roses and lost his head in 1469. The castle subsequently passed to the earls of Worcester (whose family name, confusingly, was Somerset). They further enlarged the castle in the late sixteenth century. The 5th Earl held it for the king during the Civil War and was one of the handful who refused to surrender even after the king was in the hands of his opponents in 1646. In fact, Raglan seems to have been the last royalist castle to surrender, and as a result was slighted by Parliamentary order and subsequently abandoned. The ruins are now in the care of Cadw and are normally open to the public.

Opposite: An eighteenth-century engraving of Raglan Castle which was destroyed after it fell to Cromwell's men. The great tower was so well built that it withstood pickaxes and had to be undermined.

Below: The Norman motte castle that stood on the site of Raglan Castle survived up to the fifteenth century when Sir William ap Thomas started work on the building seen in this engraving.

RICHMOND

When William the Conqueror invaded England in 1066, he was biting off more than he expected to chew. Defeat of Harold and coronation at Westminster did not subdue the English. That task took five years, and involved the displacement of the vast majority of English landholders by Normans. The final decisive act, following a second revolt in 1069 by the northern earls, aided by Danes and Welsh, was his 'harrying of the North', a campaign of atrocities in which, it was said, 'no house was left standing' between York and Durham. Much of the North Riding of Yorkshire was virtually depopulated. Thus when the Conqueror bestowed the lands of the conquered Earl Edwin of Mercia on Alan Rufus, or 'the Red' (who incidentally was a Breton, not a Norman, a relationship that caused problems of allegiance later), it was necessary to rebuild a town like Richmond, at the foot of Swaledale, virtually from scratch. Even the name is French.

Though not without anxious times and violent incidents, the history of Richmond, one of the most attractive of North Yorkshire towns, is marked by no comparable disaster. It benefited from the eminence of its feudal overlord, at various times the king himself. It was an important communications centre—and remained so until the days of the motorways—and was thus a major market, with four annual fairs during the Middle Ages. The market, grouped in a circle around a 200-year-old obelisk erected in the most prosperous days of the wool business, is still busy nowadays. A charming little Georgian theatre, recently restored to its original use, is another survivor from those days.

The castle of Alan Rufus stands high on a rocky cliff above the River Swale. The dimensions of the site explain the unusual layout of the castle, whose walls form a triangle enclosing a large bailey. It was begun in 1071, which makes it one of the earliest castles to be built in stone. Major parts of the eleventh-century walls, with flanking rectangular towers, remain on two sides of the triangle, the third side being defended by a sharp drop to the river. The building known as Scolland's Hall, after Alan of Brittany's steward, which occupies the south-eastern corner, also dates from the eleventh century. The hall was on the upper storey—the normal pattern—with the ground floor occupied by

---

Opposite: The Great Keep of Richmond Castle still stands proudly overlooking the surrounding town.

Below: Some idea of Richmond Castle's dominant position overlooking the town and the River Swale can be had from this eighteenth-century plan of the castle.

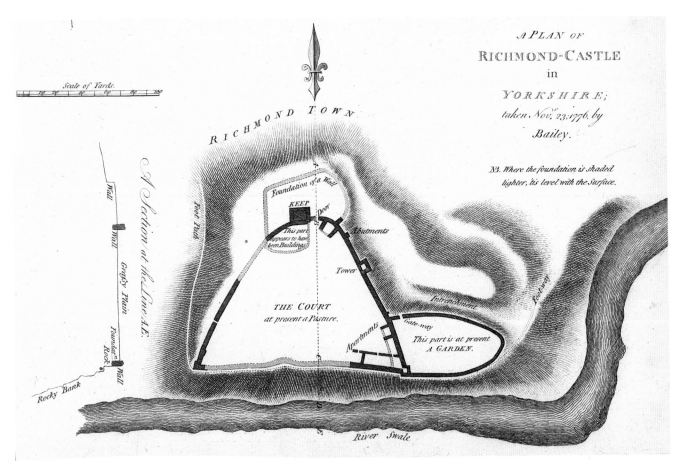

storerooms. Some rebuilding took place in the thirteenth century, perhaps after a fire of which signs can be detected on the older masonry, that apparently destroyed adjoining buildings. One of the surviving wall towers, now known as the Robin Hood Tower and partly rebuilt in the fourteenth century, once briefly held prisoner King William the Lion. The King of Scots was captured at Alnwick in 1174 after failing to enforce his claim to the earldom of Northumberland, the rejection of this claim by the English King Henry II being possibly the cause of the first formal anti-English alliance of the Scots and the French. Another interesting tower is the so-called Gold Hole Tower, containing an interesting example of early medieval latrines. Visitors are likely to prefer the more modern conveniences installed for their relief.

The most striking building, however, is the great tower which stands at the apex of the triangle, above the town and commanding marvellous views of dale and vale. This splendid structure, over 100 feet high, was built in the twelfth century (though the upper part is later), replacing the original gatehouse.

Its situation explains its remarkably peaceful history. Though sometimes confiscated, then later restored, it suffered no damage in the feudal conflicts of the Middle Ages and the turmoil of civil wars passed it by. It never seems to have been attacked at all, and its present ruined state is due not to seige or gunfire or the vengeance of Cromwell but to simple neglect. Early in the sixteenth century, when it was held by the Crown, surveyors found it in a shocking state, though their recommendations regarding immediate necessary repairs fell on deaf ears. Some minimal restoration occurred in the eighteenth century, but in the nineteenth it was being used for inappropriate purposes and unsightly utilitarian buildings were put up against the walls. It passed into the protection of the Ministry of Works in 1910, and a proper scheme of restoration was then set in motion.

Opposite: It is surprising that a castle as imposing as Richmond had such a peaceful history, the reason being that it lay well away from the principal lines of communication in medieval times.

Below: The great tower of Richmond Castle was built as an extension of the original gate tower and reached 100 feet in height.

ROCHESTER

There is a monument to Charles Dickens in Rochester Cathedral and the city is full of literary memories. For example, Restoration House, so named because Charles II stayed there on his way to reclaim the throne in 1660, was the model for Miss Havisham's house in *Great Expectations*; Eastgate House appears in *Edwin Drood*, which Dickens wrote when living at Gad's Hill (also remembered as the place where Falstaff failed to dispose of an open-ended number of assailants).

The city's long history is due to its situation at what was the lowest fordable point of the River Medway, where Watling Street (the London–Dover road) crossed it—by a bridge in late Roman times. The cathedral was founded by St Augustine himself in 604, destroyed by the Danes and rebuilt by Bishop Gundulf, who also built the castle, in the late eleventh century.

Much of Gundulf's curtain wall, and remnants of the Roman wall that preceded it, still stand, but the outstanding feature of Rochester is the great tower or keep, perhaps the finest surviving building of its type in England. It was built after 1127, when the castle was bestowed on William de Corbeil, Archbishop of Canterbury, and his successors. It is almost square in plan, about seventy feet along each wall, with towers at the corners and a solid forebuilding protecting the entrance on the north side. The walls, 12 feet thick at the ground, rise 113 feet to the parapet, with the flanking towers adding another 12 feet to the total height.

In 1215 the castle, held by rebel barons against King John, was the object of one of the best-known sieges in English history, when the south-east tower was successfully mined, with the aid of forty pigs used as firelighters to fire the timbers supporting the sappers' tunnel. Having breached the keep, the attackers were held up by the central internal wall, and the garrison held out a short time longer before being

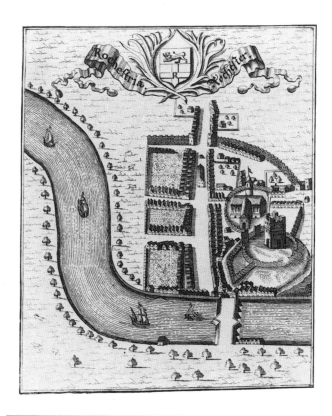

Above: J. C. Beer's plan of Rochester (*c.*1690) clearly shows the rectangular great tower of Rochester Castle which was built between 1127 and 1142.

Opposite: Building work on the rectangular great tower at Rochester Castle was begun *c.*1127. By the time this engraving was made, the rest of the castle lay in ruins leaving only the menacing Norman keep and some walling intact.

starved into surrender. The castle was restored, and a round tower replaced the casualty in the south-east corner, but forty-nine years later it came under siege again, this time from Simon de Montfort. Restored again under Edward III, it suffered further damage during the Peasants' Revolt of 1381, but was patched up by Richard II. Thereafter it gradually decayed, narrowly avoiding total demolition in the eighteenth century, but was rescued by the city corporation in the late nineteenth century. It is now preserved by English Heritage.

SKIPTON

Skipton is one of the liveliest market towns in the West Riding of Yorkshire. The sheep and cattle markets may not be what they were, but instead the town today seems to have a cultural festival of one kind or another at every season—music in the spring, painting in summer and drama in autumn. The capital of the old district of Craven, Skipton is one of those towns, like Rome, to which all roads seem to lead, due to its position commanding the Craven gaps through the Pennines. It stands on the River Aire, whose trans-Pennine passage is also exploited by the Liverpool–Leeds Canal. The Normans built an earthwork castle on the site of the present one, at the end of the High Street and above the river, which guards one side. The first stone buildings were put up in the late twelfth century, though there are few remains of that period.

King Edward II bestowed the castle—a brief tenure—on his unpopular favourite, Piers Gaveston, but Skipton is primarily associated with the Clifford family, who took their name from Clifford in Herefordshire though their estates were mainly in Yorkshire. The barony of Skipton was in their possession from the late thirteenth to the late seventeenth centuries, and what we see today is mainly due to the last of the line, Lady Anne, Countess Dowager of Pembroke. She restored both the castle and the fourteenth-century church next to it in the 1650s, after the castle had withstood a somewhat half-hearted siege during the Civil War and had afterwards been slighted by Parliamentary forces. The Cliffords, now earls of Cumberland, were no longer great warlords like their ancestors, but they were royalists; the king appointed the current earl, who was more scholar than soldier, his Lieutenant of the North. The Earl of Pembroke, on the other hand, supported Parliament; his death in 1650 allowed Anne to return to Skipton and begin its restoration, a task commemorated in an inscription over the entrance.

The castle, built mainly of limestone from a local quarry, has thick curtain walls interspersed with hefty round towers, and a four-towered gatehouse, the dominant building. Much of the domestic buildings from the early fourteenth century, including a hall some fifty feet long, survive on the north side of the courtyard, though the general appearance is rather of the Renaissance. The militancy of the battlements crowning the octagonal tower of 1536 is belied by the large windows below.

Opposite: An eleventh-century earthwork castle stood on the site now occupied by the splendid Skipton Castle. There have been considerable renovations and additions since the Civil War when it was badly damaged.

Below: The twin-drum towered gatehouse of Skipton Castle carries the inscription *'Désormais'* meaning 'Henceforth' that marks the restoration work undertaken by the Countess Dowager of Pembroke in the seventeenth century.

STIRLING

When Agricola embanked on the conquest of Scotland in AD 83, he made his base at Stirling. Like the rival kings of Scots and English in later times, he recognized its significance as 'the key to the North'. Commanding the Forth valley, Stirling was crucial, perhaps a more important stronghold than Edinburgh itself, and during the Wars of Independence it changed hands frequently. Wallace had a great victory at Stirling Bridge in 1297, commemorated by a lofty monument. The castle fell to Edward I in 1304 in a famous siege, which was possibly organized by the renowned George of St James and included the use of Greek fire (a device learned by the Crusaders in Byzantium). The English held it for the next ten years, while all other strongholds were falling to the Bruce, and Edward II's desire to relieve the besieged garrison in 1314 prompted his disastrous march to Bannockburn, a mile or two south.

Stirling continued to play a crucial role under the Stewart dynasty, several of whom were born or crowned (or both) there, and at times it was virtually a second capital. During this period, it changed in character. Despite the unsettled times which led to more violent events at Stirling during the sixteenth century, by then it had long been more of a royal palace than a fortress. Possibly its finest ornament is the great hall built by Robert Cochrane for James III in the fifteenth century, closely followed by the gatehouse and palace buildings of James IV and James V. The nearby church of the Holy Rude, where Mary Queen of Scots was crowned, was for nearly three centuries divided in two as the result of a local quarrel. In the Civil War Stirling was dominated by the Covenanters; the castle was taken by General Monk in 1651. The Campbells held it in the Jacobite Rebellion in 1715 and Prince Charles Edward attacked it unavailingly in 1746.

Stirling Castle has obvious affinities with Edinburgh (p 72), and is built on a similar site—on a high, in places sheer, basalt rock that dominates the city. Like Edinburgh too, the buildings that make up the castle complex today are relatively recent. There is scarcely anything here older than the fifteenth century: the castle captured by Edward I was probably wooden. The Act of Union (1603) reduced the significance of Stirling, as of Edinburgh, but the former city never experienced a great expansion like Edinburgh's in the eighteenth century.

Opposite: The history of Stirling Castle is steeped in the history of the Stuart family, from James II who was born there in 1430, to Bonnie Prince Charlie whose men took Stirling but failed to storm the castle during the rising of 1745.

Below: Stirling Castle looks today very much as it did when this engraving was done. The town, though, has grown and now sprawls all round the escarpment on which the castle sits.

TANTALLON

The spectacular ruins of Tantallon Castle, in local, reddish stone befitting the old stronghold of the Red Douglases, overlook the Firth of Forth. Directly opposite, little more than a mile away, a distinctive form emerges from the sea; Bass Rock, the remains of the plug of an ancient volcano, about 350 feet high and a mile in circumference. Today a nature reserve, it was the last place in Britain to acknowledge King William III: a small party of Jacobites seized the Rock in 1691 and held out for the banished James II until 1694. Contemplating these juxtaposed strongpoints, one made by Nature the other by Man, the perceptive photographer's eye of Christina Gascoigne led her to remark on the comparative fragility of the latter, a ruin after four centuries while the Bass Rock has remained virtually unchanged for millennia.

The castle, featured in Sir Walter Scott's novel *Marmion*, is situated on a rocky promontory, about three miles east of what is now the resort town of North Berwick (golf and bracing breezes). Protected by the sea and steep cliffs on three sides, the site was made virtually into an island by the digging of ditches across the promontory. Though a fine defensive position when the castle was built in the late fourteenth century, rising ground inland made it less than ideal when artillery came of age. There may well have been a previous stronghold here, but the present castle was probably built by the 1st Earl of Douglas. It was certainly in Douglas hands early in the fifteenth century, and remained their property until the end of the seventeenth century, when it was abandoned. As the Douglas earls of Angus were during much of that period among the most powerful forces in Scotland—powerful enough at times to play off the king of Scots against the king of England and vice-versa, though not always to their own ultimate benefit—Tantallon figures prominently in Scottish history. It held some famous prisoners, including Alexander, Lord of the Isles, in 1429. The notorious 5th Earl of Angus ('Bell-the-Cat'—the expression he used concerning his arbitrary execution of several royal courtiers) was besieged by James IV in 1491, though that didn't stop him becoming Chancellor the next year. James V seized the castle in 1529. General Monk took it after a twelve-day siege in 1651, and thereafter ruin set in. The most impressive remains consist of a mighty curtain wall with flanking towers, centred on a gatehouse.

Opposite: A century before this engraving was made, General Monk laid seige to Tantallon Castle which held out for twelve days before surrendering. It then fell into disrepair.

Below: Even in ruins, Tantallon Castle, built in dramatic red freestone, presents an imposing face to the world.

TINTAGEL

Tintagel is a spectacular spot, high on the rocky cliffs of a promontory projecting into the sea on the north Cornish coast. The castle must have looked spectacular too, once upon a time, but only the barest ruins remain. Part of it was washed away by the Atlantic towards the end of the Middle Ages, and what was left was abandoned to the forces of nature. What remains to be seen now was rescued in the nineteenth century and has since been properly looked after.

The castle was founded in the twelfth century and enlarged in the thirteenth by the royal earls of Cornwall. The Black Prince is said to have rebuilt the great hall, and there was more rebuilding after him. But the castle, which was not particularly significant strategically, has played little part in history since then. One reason why the site interested our Victorian ancestors so much was its link with legends much older. For Tintagel is associated with a hero, British not English, who looms even larger than the Black Prince. This is the legendary King Arthur, a figure who belongs to literature and mythology rather than history. No doubt the legend had some authentic origin (legends nearly always do), and there is strong evidence to substantiate the existence of a Romano-British chieftain who led resistance to the invading Saxons in the late fifth century. Still, from a purely historical point of view, King Arthur is a distinctly overinflated figure. His connection with Tintagel is also more tenuous than one may suppose, depending on a not very reliable chronicle written over 600 years after his time.

However, it must be admitted that Tintagel bears evidence of settlement long before the castle was founded. Somewhere here was the cell of a Celtic missionary, St Juliot, who would probably have been a fairly close contemporary of 'Arthur'. The remains exist of little, squarish, stone houses which were the homes of a religious community, deriving from St Juliot's habitation here and still in existence in the ninth century.

Apart from the mysterious Celtic mists that surround the place, Tintagel has another historic, perhaps unique, claim to fame. Before the Reform Act of 1832 it had two Members of Parliament but only one qualified voter—the vicar.

Opposite: Before the Victorians set about restoring the remains of Tintagel, local quarries and the storms of 400 winters saw to it that what was left of the castle after it was abandoned in the fifteenth century became almost totally dilapidated.

Below: A dramatic engraving of Tintagel Castle and its spectacular position on the rocky cliffs of the north Cornish coast.

TINTAGELL CASTLE
CORNWALL

TOWER OF LONDON

The town of London was founded by the Romans, the area roughly corresponding to the famous 'square mile' of the City today. They built a wall around it, which was restored by King Alfred in the ninth century, and in 1066 William the Conqueror chose as the site of his most famous castle the south-eastern corner of that wall, abutting the River Thames.

The White Tower, the original Norman castle, has not changed very much in nine centuries, apart from the dubious onion domes and the windows—enlarged by Sir Christopher Wren in the late seventeenth century. The remainder of this, one of the greatest medieval fortresses in Europe, which occupies twelve acres within the walls, dates mainly from the thirteenth century, though considerable alterations and additions have been made in every century. In Henry III's reign the White Tower was whitewashed—hence the now incongruous name.

The history of the Tower is as long as it is grisly. It has served a great variety of purposes. It was a royal palace (coronation processions started from here) until Cromwell dismantled the royal apartments in the 1650s. It was an arsenal and fortress, functions it still retains in modified form, and for over 400 years it housed the Royal Mint. From 1235 it was also a zoo, begun when the Emperor Frederick II gave Henry III three leopards. After a lion attacked some soldiers in 1834 the animals were moved to Regent's Park. Above all, the Tower was a prison, especially for 'traitors', over fifty of whom were executed on Tower Hill or, less publicly, Tower Green. The evidence of their presence can still be seen in pathetic scratchings on the walls of the various towers where they were incarcerated. The princes who disappeared in 1483 were probably held in the Bloody Tower, although that name was not applied to it until some time later: it was formerly known, less descriptively, as the Garden Tower. The future Queen Elizabeth I was held for two months in the Bell Tower—earlier the final residence of Bishop Fisher and Sir Thomas More—by her suspicious sister, Mary. When, still in custody, she left the Tower, gunners fired an unauthorized salute as her barge passed by.

The condemned entered by boat through the grim maw of what is now called Traitors Gate, and the fearful noise of the water rushing though the portcullis as the tide went out did not help their peace of mind (the noisome moat was drained in 1843 and sown with grass). It is pleasant to recall that not all of them ended up headless under the turf of Tower Green (or, if sufficiently notable, in the twelfth century chapel of St Peter ad Vincula). The Jacobite Lord Nithsdale slipped away the night before his execution in 1716 disguised as a

Opposite: Nineteenth-century Londoners are seen going about their everyday business in the shadow of the Tower. Today, the Tower attracts more than one million visitors every year.

Below: Established by William the Conqueror in 1067, the Tower of London's history is long and colourful and it has played a major part in the history of Britain.

girl. He had better luck than another escapee (there were not many), the Welsh prince, son of Llywelyn the Great, who fell to his death in an attempt in 1244.

During the Middle Ages the Tower was twice surrendered to opposing forces. In 1215 it was besieged by the rebellious barons, and King John handed it over, though more as a politic gesture than because it was in danger of falling. During the Peasants' Revolt of 1381 it was taken by Wat Tyler and a handful of Kentish men, who seem to have walked in, no doubt with Fifth-Column assistance. They treated the apprehensive knights of the garrison jovially, if irreverently, but finding the Archbishop of Canterbury hiding in the chapel, dragged him out and chopped off his head.

Prisoners, including Roger Casement and Rudolph Hess, have been held in the Tower occasionally in recent times and a dozen spies were shot there during World War II, when bombs and a couple of doodle-bugs caused considerable damage, but since Queen Victoria's day it has become primarily a museum and national monument. The Crown Jewels, originally housed in the Martin Tower (whence the

bold Colonel Blood attempted to steal them in 1671) but now in a secure vault below the nineteenth-century Wellington Barracks, are the greatest tourist attraction but the unsurpassed collection of armour and weapons is also of great interest. It includes Henry VIII's codpiece, in which childless women used to stick pins in the hope that they would conceive. That is now discouraged, but some old traditions are maintained—the uniforms of the Yeomen Warders or 'Beefeaters'; the nightly ceremony of the Keys, which dates back 700 years and the feeding of the ravens, whose departure from the Tower will foretell its fall.

Opposite: The area around the Tower is now completely built up, the roads are clogged with traffic but otherwise very little about the Tower of London has changed from this depiction of it during the reign of Elizabeth I.

Below: Queen Elizabeth I was on the throne when this plan of London was drawn (Braun and Hogenberg, *c*.1572). Only eighteen years earlier she had been a prisoner in the Tower, held on suspicion of being involved in a plot to overthrow her sister, Mary Tudor.

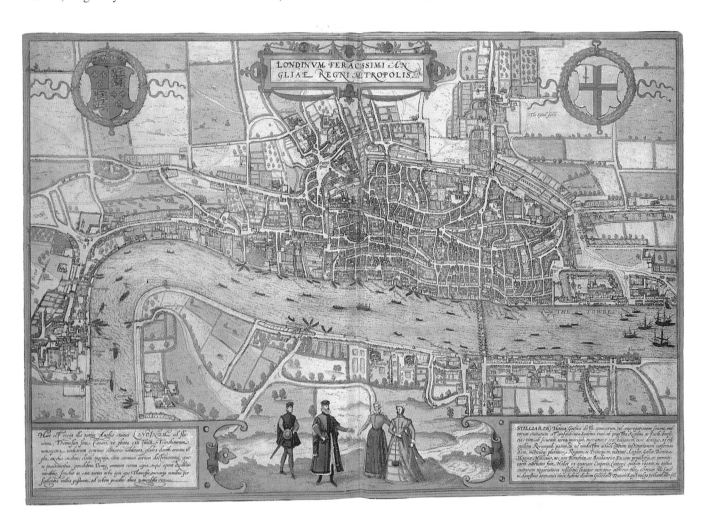

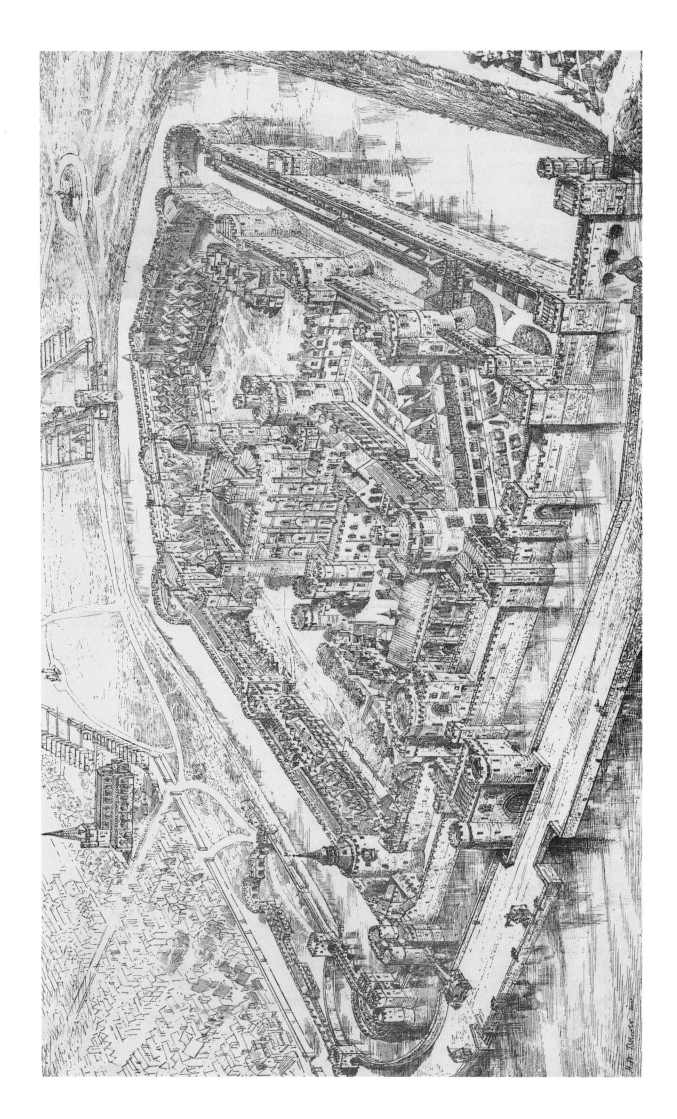

WARKWORTH

As the salmon, fewer and smaller than of old, make their way up the River Coquet in Northumbria bound for the spawning places in the Cheviots, they must take a sharp northward loop a mile from the harbour, encompassing the old village of Warkworth with its Norman church, fourteenth-century towered bridge, ruined castle and, reached by boat from the castle, the Hermitage carved partly out of the rock, which is the subject of an old ballad of the Percies.

The castle is of special interest both for its history, a stormy one like that of most castles in this region, and for the unusual, almost unique, design of the main tower or keep. Its early history is obscure, though its origins as a motte and bailey castle are still obvious. It was not much of a stronghold in 1173, when it was taken easily by William the Lion, repulsed at Alnwick (p 14) ten miles north. The Percies of Alnwick took possession of Warkworth in 1332: their heraldic lion may still be seen on the vault of the Lion Tower, which formed the entrance to the hall in the bailey. They were responsible for replacing the twelfth-century stone tower with the present building (there were minor alterations—the usual enlarged windows and so on—later). In plan, this building consists of a thick cross imposed on a smaller square, so that the arms of the cross extend beyond the sides of the square. As all projecting angles are mitred off, the line of the walls changes direction thirty-two times.

A central watch tower rises above the level of the walls. The south side is enclosed by the curtain wall around the bailey, with gatehouse in the south. The polygonal Grey Mare's Tail Tower in the east was built about the same time as the keep and echoes its form; it is remarkable for the height of its arrow loops—sixteen feet.

The Percies, though the king's chief lieutenants in the North, were practically independent magnates, and were not always to be found on the side of the Crown. The rebellion

Above: The Hermitage at Warkworth Castle is partly carved out of rock and access to it can only be gained by boat from the castle.

Opposite: Warkworth Castle with its multi-angular great tower built for Henry Percy dominates the loop on the River Coquet upon which it stands.

against Henry IV, well-known through Shakespeare's depiction of it, was planned at Warkworth. After the Revolt of the Northern Earls against Elizabeth in 1569, Warkworth Castle was apparently deserted. It is now maintained by English Heritage.

WARWICK

The old county town of Warwickshire escaped almost entirely the excesses of the Industrial Revolution which transformed the region to the north, and it remains a small, attractive borough with many seventeenth- and eighteenth-century buildings and a sprinkling even older, including the half-timbered Leycester Hospital, originally a fifteenth-century guildhall, with its galleried courtyard. The history of Warwick goes back at least to the early ninth century, and at the time of the Domesday survey it contained 225 households. Commanding a crossing of the River Avon, it was fortified by Aethelflaed, 'the Lady of the Mercians', about 914, and the motte known as 'Aethelflaed's Mound', at the southern corner of the present castle, supported a fort of some kind when William the Conqueror arrived in Warwick in 1068. There are traces of a twelfth-century shell keep but, as it stands today, the castle dates mainly from a major reconstruction in the fourteenth century. Some additions were made by one of the most famous earls of Warwick, Richard Neville, the power broker of the Wars of the Roses nicknamed 'Kingmaker'.

The magnificent state of the castle is due largely to Fulke Greville, poet and statesman, who received it from James I in 1604. He converted it at enormous expense into a palace, and it remained the seat of his successors, earls of Warwick, until 1978, when it was sold to Madame Tussauds. Although completely changed inside, the exterior is still that of a late medieval enclosure castle, the single most striking feature being Caesar's Tower, in the north-east, which is on the plan of a clover leaf and stands over 130 feet (six storeys) high. It is matched by the polygonal Guy's Tower in the north-west.

The contents are of no less interest. Here is the great two-handed sword allegedly wielded by the tenth-century hero, Guy of Warwick, though in fact it postdates him by at least 300 years. Other armour includes the head-piece of a war horse, again associated with Guy but probably dating from the Wars of the Roses, and a silver-mounted targe (shield) presented by Bonnie Prince Charlie. The most famous object is the Warwick Vase, a huge Roman ceremonial vase in white marble, retrieved by Sir William Hamilton, husband of Lord Nelson's Emma, from a lake at the Villa Hadrian at Tivoli and sold to the Earl of Warwick.

Opposite: Warwick is a fine example of a natural site overlooking a river. A Saxon fort once stood on the banks of the River Avon now occupied by the castle, the chief midlands stronghold of 'Kingmaker' Warwick.

Below: In 1820 when this engraving was made, Warwick Castle looked very much as it did when Earl Beauchamp completed the building work he embarked on in the late fourteenth century.

WINDSOR

A Saxon royal residence existed at Old Windsor, but William I built his castle in a different manor, two miles to the north-west, on a loop of the River Thames. The original motte castle formed one of the many strategic strongpoints placed around London.

Old Windsor dwindled in importance as New Windsor grew up around the castle, on which it was wholly dependent. After the building of the railways, the town expanded greatly, but is today predominantly Victorian in appearance although it retains some older buildings of interest, including Nell Gwynne's house and the guildhall. This building was completed by the young Christopher Wren, who was instructed by his nervous and sceptical clients to insert pillars on the ground floor for fear the ceiling would collapse. He agreed, but with characteristic irony so placed them that they have, in fact, no structural significance. The ceiling has not fallen.

Windsor castle has been a royal residence for the best part of a millennium and is therefore unique. In plan, the figure-of-eight outline, stretching about half a mile from east to west, reflects the twelfth-century castle—a central motte surmounted later by the famous Round Tower or keep—with a bailey on either side. The narrow central part forms the middle ward, with the lower ward, containing St George's Chapel and the modern entrance (Henry VIII's Gate), to the west, and the upper ward, containing the private and state apartments, to the east.

Some authorities maintain that the Norman castle was built in stone from the start, but it is uncertain how much had been completed before the reign of Henry II. He was the second founder of Windsor, who built spacious royal apartments and began the enclosure wall and towers. Some damage was done in the reign of John, when the castle was twice besieged by the barons. It was not taken, and never suffered another siege. Henry III restored and expanded the buildings, and Edward III, born here, carried out further alterations and additions. He founded St George's Chapel for his Knights of the Garter, though the present, famously

Opposite: With its centuries-long royal connections, Berkshire is officially known as 'The Royal County of Berkshire' hence the royal coat of arms decorating the title of this map by Thomas Moule.

Below: A view of Windsor Castle as seen from the River Thames. It has been the principle residence of British sovereigns since the eleventh century and is now the largest inhabited castle in Europe.

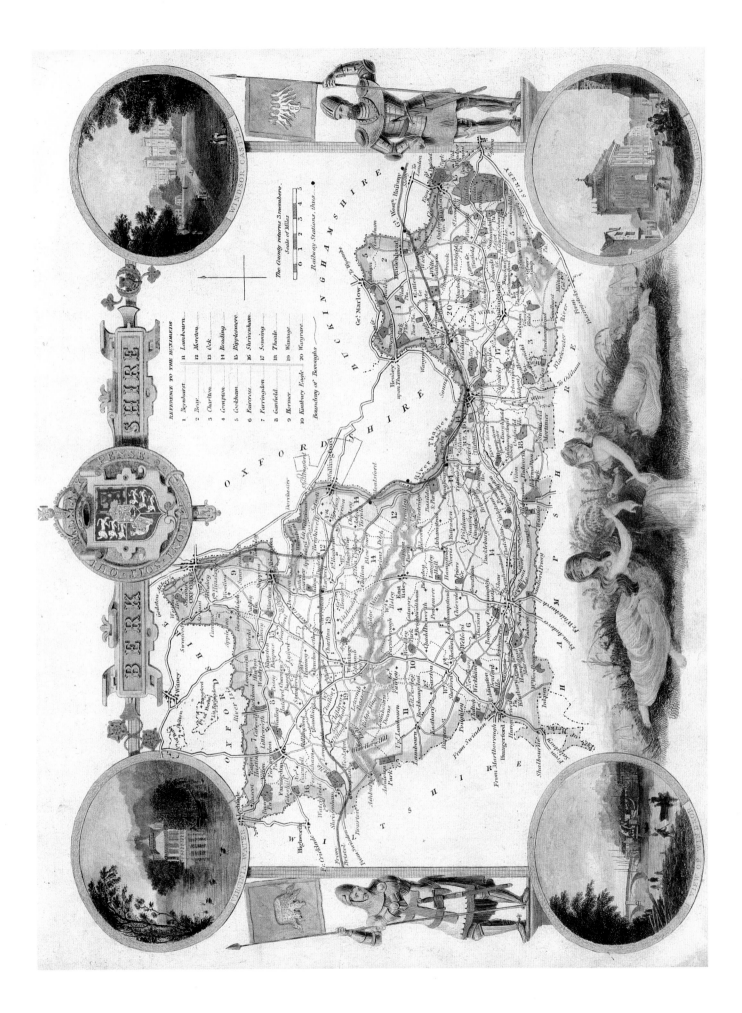

beautiful chapel dates from 1528. Besides being a fortress and a palace, Windsor was also a prison, and the kings of three countries languished here, the last being a king of England, Charles I.

Further additions and alterations were made frequently in the course of the centuries. They included an occupation by Parliamentary forces, who melted down some medieval royal armour among other acts of vandalism during the Civil War, and extensive work under Charles II. Every monarch had plans for improving Windsor, but the biggest reconstruction took place during the reign of George IV. His architect was Sir Jeffrey Wyatville who raised the Round Tower by over thirty feet to its present dominance, rebuilt the royal apartments, and created many of the present splendours, including the Waterloo Chamber which is still used by the Queen for state banquets. Looking at the castle from the river, what you see is nearly all his work: pre-Wyatville prints reveal the enormous difference.

Though a good man for battlements and machicolations, Wyatville was apparently less successful with domestic arrangements. The drainage was such that Queen Victoria found parts of the castle uninhabitable even after the old cesspools had been obliterated in 1840. Bathrooms were not abundant either.

Though never troubled by the roar of the aircraft departing Heathrow (under current bylaws her great-great-grandaughter is entitled to apply for a grant for double-glazing), Queen Victoria had security tightened up after some visitors took one of her sketchbooks and published its contents.

Security today is tighter still, though generally unobtrusive. Parts of the castle are naturally not open to the public, and what *is* open varies according to the activities of the royals. However, there is always plenty to see even if Leonardo's drawings, or Queen Mary's Edwardian dolls' house are not available. A disastrous fire—not the first in the castle's history—destroyed the north-east corner in 1992, though practically all the valuable contents were saved.

Opposite: The land occupied by the Great Park that surrounds Windsor Castle was once a royal hunting forest. Anyone who dared to hunt there or even to fell a tree risked execution. Happily, the park is now open to the public. This painting by Paul Sandby shows the castle from Mother Dod's Hill in the south-east of the park.

Below: Although interesting in its detail, a simple ground plan of Windsor Castle cannot do justice to the scale and magnificence of this fortified palace. It extends for over half a mile overlooking the River Thames and can be seen for miles around.

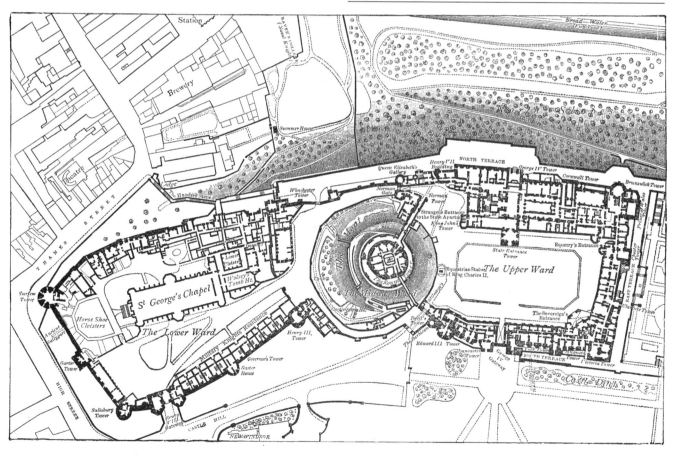

YORK

The size of London and a relatively effective central government inhibited the development of great provincial cities in England, but York, the capital of the North, is one. The Romans observed the strategic importance of the site and built a large fort there, of which some remnants may still be seen. It became the northern ecclesiastical capital in the seventh century, and still holds that position today as seat of the Church of England's second-ranking archbishop. Conquered by the Danes in the ninth century it developed into the most prosperous town of the Danelaw.

William the Conqueror's campaign of vengeance in the North brought disaster to York. However, William saw it as a vital command centre and erected two motte-and-bailey castles bracketing the river. One was soon destroyed: recent excavations revealed traces of it on Baile Hill. The other, on the site of the present Clifford's Tower, was burned in 1190 during a notorious massacre of the Jews.

York recovered rapidly and became one of the richest cities in England during the Middle Ages, with commercial connections, especially in the wool trade, throughout north-west Europe. The city walls—gates and walls are largely intact—ran for nearly three miles and enclosed over sixty churches and religious foundations, above all the great minster. The castle was rebuilt in the thirteenth century and was an important base during the wars with Scotland. The tower, known as Clifford's Tower after Roger de Clifford who was hanged from the walls in 1322, is built on an unusual quatrefoil, or four-leaf, plan (probably French-inspired) on a high motte. It is well preserved, though little remains of the curtain wall and towers of the bailey.

With the sixteenth-century Reformation, York entered a decline, due mainly to its decreasing importance as an inland port and the gradual loss of the wool trade. However, it remained the chief communications centre of the north—it was a favourite stopping place for long distance coach travellers—and in the nineteenth century it became a great railway centre, aided by the ambitions of one of its most notable citizens, George Hudson, 'the Railway King'. Today, York still attracts many visitors. To its credit, the city's presentation of its own past through museums and exhibitions as well as buildings, is second to none; the Viking town is presented with special vividness.

Opposite: This Tallis map of York suggests that when it was drawn (*c*.1855) more of the castle was standing than can be seen today when all that remains is the tower named after Lord Robert Clifford, who was hanged in chains there in 1322.

Below: After the castle in York on which Clifford's Tower now stands was destroyed in 1190, the motte was raised to its present height of sixty feet.

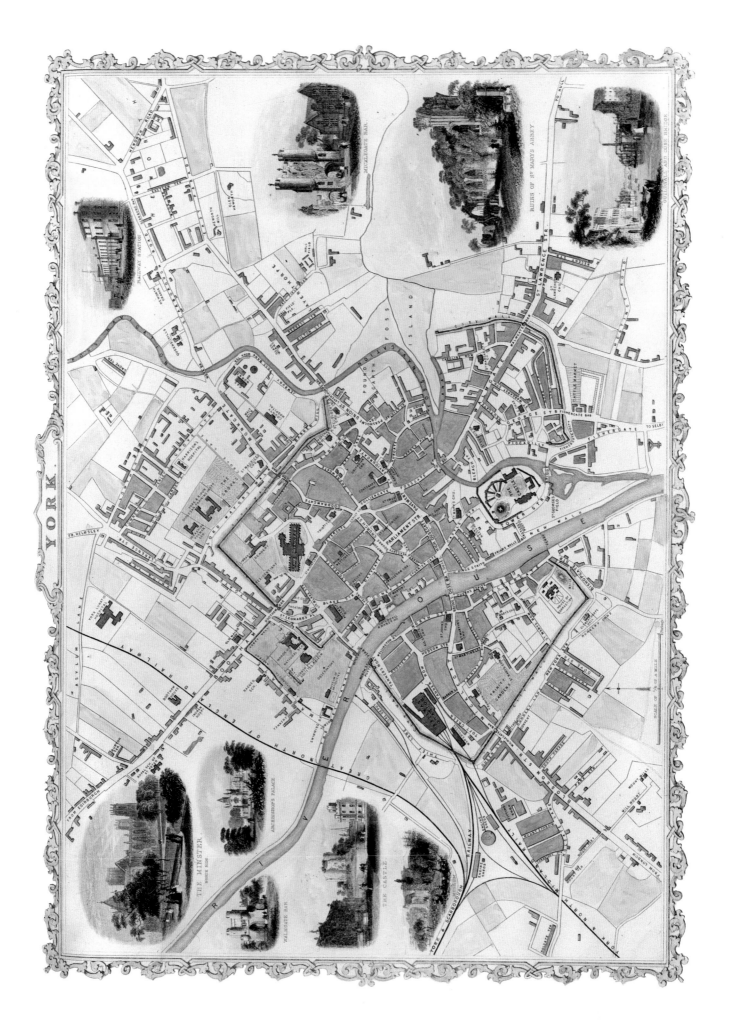

YORK.

MICKLEGATE BAR.

RUINS OF ST MARY'S ABBEY.

THE MINSTER. SOUTH SIDE.

ARCHBISHOP'S PALACE.

WALMGATE BAR.

THE CASTLE.

BIBLIOGRAPHY

DAVISON, B. K., *Castles, Observer's series (1986)*

FRY, P. S., *Castles of the British Isles (1990)*

GASCOIGNE, B. and C., *Castles of Britain (1975)*

HARRIS, N., *Castles of England, Scotland and Wales (1991)*

HARVEY, J., *English Medieval Architects (1984)*

JOHNSON, P., *Castles of England, Scotland and Wales (1989)*

LINDSAY, M., *Castles of Scotland (1986)*

McNEILL, R., *English Heritage Book of Castles (1990)*

OMAN, Sir C., *British Castles (1990)*

TAYLOR, A. J., *The Welsh Castles of Edward I (1986)*

PICTURE ACKNOWLEDGEMENTS

The Publishers would like to thank the following for their kind permission to
reproduce the images that appear on the pages listed below:-

Bridgeman Art Library, London: 125

Derek Forss: 17, 29, 37, 67.

*The Mansell Collection, London: 25, 30, 31, 48, 57, 59, 60, 61, 62, 69, 85, 99, 100,
101, 102, 106, 108, 109, 111, 112, 114, 115, 117, 124, 126.*

Jonathan Potter Ltd., London: 23, 40, 64, 86, 92, 104.

Spectrum Colour Library, London: 6, 49, 79, 93, 107, 121.

Thanks are due to Mrs Lorna Maund and Flick for their hand-colouring.